Patrice Cole
Jennifer Wallens
Suzanne Grace
Nicki Love
Patti Negri
Sunhee Park
Chinhee Park
Gabriela Castillo
Reverend Claire Braddock
Reverend Marla Phillips
Reverend Christa Urban
Syd Saeed

In recognition of their outstanding contributions to the supernatural and spiritual world

Copyright ©2012 by Maximillien de Lafayette. All rights reserved. No part of this book may be used or reproduced by any means, graphic, electronic, or mechanical, including photocopying, recording, taping or by any information storage retrieval system without the written permission of the author except in the case of brief quotations embodied in critical articles and reviews.

Published by Times Square Press, and WJNA, Inc. New York.
United States of America.
Date of Publication: March 5, 2012

Author's website: www.maximilliendelafayettebibliography.com
Author's book on spirituality, mediumship, healing, remote viewing, psychic abilities and supernatural powers.
http://maximilliendelafayettebibliography.com/spirituality.htm
Author's bookstore: http://stores.lulu.com/maximilliendelafayette
Contact: delafayette6@aol.com
This book is available in paperback at lulu.com and in Kindle edition at amazon.com.
Other books by Maximillien de Lafayette are available nationwide and worldwide, including the Nook edition at Barnes and Noble.

How to Become an Enlightened Psychic Detective and Remote Viewer
Ulema Psychometry Lessons, Training & Techniques to locate Missing People and Identifying Places & Objects
Book 3 from a set of 4 books

An Official Publication/Handbook of the
American Federation of Certified Psychics and Mediums

***   ***   ***

New Books by Maximillien de Lafayette in these fields:
Supernatural, Paranormal, Psychic studies, Mediumship, Remote Viewing, Healing, Energy, Tarot, Fortune-Telling, Clairvoyance
See products' details on page 137

Maximillien de Lafayette

HOW TO BECOME AN ENLIGHTENED PSYCHIC DETECTIVE AND REMOTE VIEWER

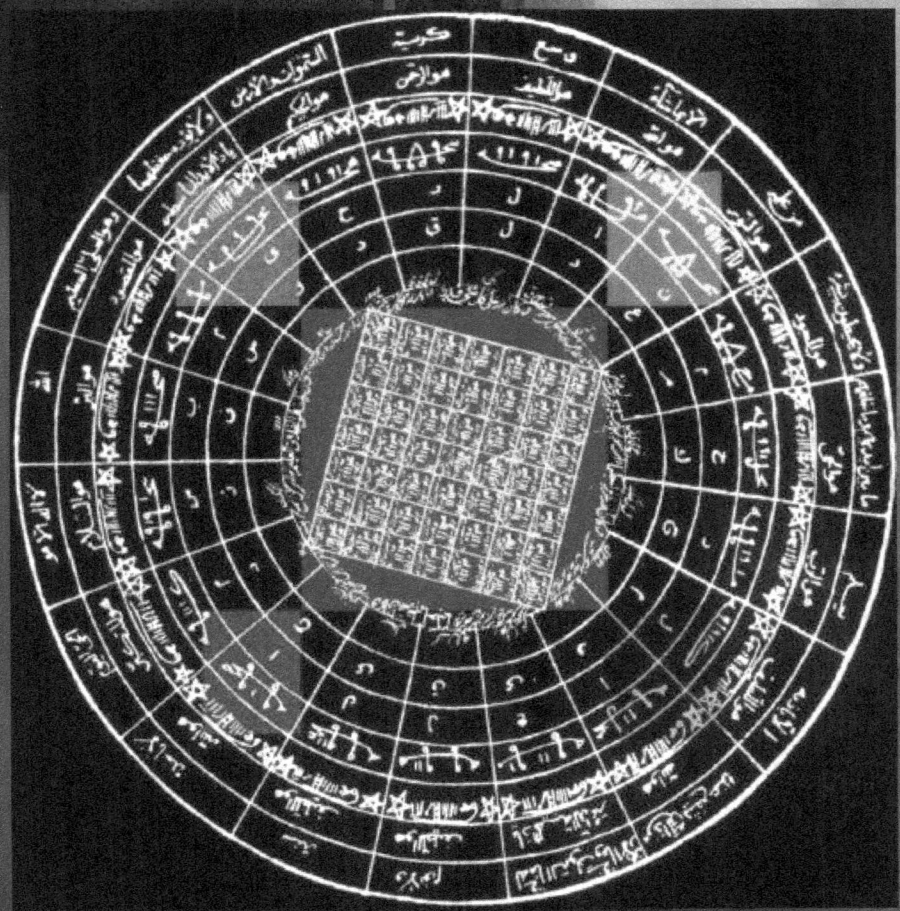

Ulema Psychometry Lessons, Training & Techniques to Locate Missing People and Identify Places & Objects

An Official Publication/Handbook of the
American Federation of Certified Psychics and Mediums

TIMES SQUARE PRESS

⌘ NOTA BENE ⌘

- To avoid all sorts of troubles and psychological confusion (s), all topics discussed in this series were approached from a philosophical-metaphysical-esoteric angle.

- Bear in mind that the Ulema's teachings and/or opinions should not be considered as a professional advice at any level – therapeutic, medical, psychological, mental health, etc. – thus avoiding any conflict with professional licensing bodies and legal practitioners in these fields.

- They are of a purely philosophical-esoteric nature.

- The Kira'ats (Readings) were given by the Ulema in Asia, and the Near/Middle East within a confined milieu of seekers of metaphysical and esoteric knowledge.

- Many of the texts as published in this book are excerpts from their Kira'ats and Rou'ya (Visions) that first appeared centuries ago, and continue to enlighten many of us.

- You enter their world at your own risk.

How to Become an Enlightened Psychic Detective and Remote Viewer

Ulema Psychometry Lessons, Training & Techniques to locate Missing People and Identifying Places & Objects
Book 3 from a set of 4 books

Based upon De Lafayette's two books on Ulema Chabariduri Technique and Chabariduri

Maximillien de Lafayette

An Official Handbook/Publication of the
American Federation of Certified Psychics and Medium

Times Square Press. WJNA, Inc.
Berlin. New York
2012

Acknowledgment and Gratitude

I am deeply grateful to the Honorable Ulema, Anunnaki-Ulema, Cheiks, Allamah, Gurus, and Asaatiza, who have guided me in this work:

Anunnaki-Ulema, The Right Honorable Cheik Al Baydani
Anunnaki-Ulema Mordachai ben Zvi
Anunnaki-Ulema Ayira Kermaat
Allamah Subhi Al Barazani
Grand Master, Ulema Dr. Farid Tayarah
Shaman Shabalah Erirou Ataneh
Allamah Kader Al Tabrizi
Allamah Shaker El Diin
Allamah Suleiman Sharaf El Diin
Allamah Cheik Talal Salem Al Badri
Allamah Cheik Khalid Al Faqueeh
Cheik Suleiman Al Habashi
Cheik Waleed Subhi Al Yamani
Allamah Cheik Ala' Alaweh Ayeelou

For without their help and guidance, this book would have remained the shadow of an idea in my drawers.

***   ***   ***

Table of Contents

A note from the publishers...12
Preface...15

Glossary/Terminology...16

Chapter I: Cadari-Rou'yaa Technique...23
- Reading the thoughts, intentions and feelings of others...23
- Definition...23
- The technique...23

Chapter II: Chabariduri Technique...31
- Learning from sensing the vibrations of objects and people at distance...31
- Definition...31
- Mystic Ulema Kiraat...32
- Stage One...32
- Stage Two...32
- Stage Three...33
- From my Kira'at at the Ma'aad...33
- Fik'r-Telemetry: Ulema psychometry...37
- I. Definition and introduction...37
- II. Objectives and purposes of these exercises...37
- You are going to identify a few things...37
- a-Objects...37
- b-Areas and places...38
- c-People...38
- III. The exercise...38
- Generalities/basic steps...39
- The mental-metaphysical process...39
- Follow these instructions...39

- Looking at the photograph of an object...40
- Illustration #1 object...40
- Illustration #2 object...41
- Illustration #3 object...43
- Illustration #4 object...45
- Looking at the photograph of a person...46
- Follow these instructions...46
- Phase one...46
- Phase two...47
- Illustration #2 person...48
- Phase three...49
- Illustration #3 person...49
- Illustration #4 person...51

Chapter III: Your Ulema psychometry and remote viewing tests start here in this chapter...53

Chapter IV: Your first reading...87
- Let's set-up the scene...87
- Reading the face of a person...87
- Instructions...87
- Seeing the aura and reading the vibes centered around the chest...91

Chapter V: Reading peoples' thoughts via lama technique...93
- I. Definition...93
- II. Synopsis of the technique...94
- Generalities...94
- III. How to use the Nizraat Takaroob technique...95
- Follow these instructions...95
- Illustration #1...95
- Step #1...95
- IV. Identifying the two positions of the triangles of the Grid...96
- Step #2...96

- Step #3...96
- Nizraat Takabroob technique...97
- Step #4...100
- Step #5...100
- Step #6...101
- Step #7...101
- Step #8...101
- Step #9...101
- Step #10...104
- Instructions for Step #10...106
- Illustration #4...109
- Step #11...110
- Step #12...111
- Step #13...114
- Step #14...114
- Step #15...114
- V. The benefits from mastering the Nizraat Takaroob technique...118

Chapter VI: The practical aspect of reading peoples' thoughts via lama technique...121
- Introduction: Generalities...121
- The technique: It works like this...122

A Note From The Publishers

This series of psychics, mediums and healers handbook of curriculum, lessons, training and techniques (Approximately 900 pages plus numerous charts) was produced as an extensive handbook and a curriculum to be used by professional psychics, mediums, healers, seers, and lightworkers. It is based upon the 250 books previously written in the fields of supernatural and paranormal by the Mystic Ulema, Maximillien de Lafayette. The series should not be considered as a "repetitious" or a "recycling work" from his previous published books and encyclopedias

To many readers, de Lafayette's work is overwhelming.
Consequently, many topics and important subjects in these fields were lost in the immensity of information, lectures and findings provided in his massive published work.
De Lafayette's work is too much, too large, and too varied; this has created some inconvenience and difficulties in finding the subjects and topics of interest to many readers, simply because they were scattered on hundreds of thousands of pages which appeared under hundreds of titles.
You do admit, that it is a hard task to find particular subjects you are interested in, without going through the entire published work of the author.
This fact has convinced us that –in the best interest of the readers and practitioners– we should provide the professional lightworkers with a concise set that leads them directly to the area (s) of their interest, and which is closely related to their practice. This set serves these purposes.

This series of three books will show you and teach you how to become an effective and enlightened medium, psychic and metaphysical healer.
It will also provide you with lessons, practical training, and step-by-step instructions on how to find, learn, develop and use esoteric techniques which produce astonishing supernatural and paranormal results; techniques and know-how which were shrouded in secrecy for thousands of years, such as:

- 1-How to effectively communicate with entities, spirits and the dead in general.
- 2-How to set up your séances.
- 3-How to summon and command spirits, entities and elements from different dimensions.
- 4-Remote viewing.
- 5-How to locate missing people.
- 6-How to develop your Supersymetric Mind.
- 7-How to enter multiple dimensions, such as non-physical dimensions, an adjacent dimension, a parallel dimension.
- 8-How to foresee future events.
- 9-How to see the Aura.
- 10-How to visit the past and the future.
- 11-How to read others' mind.
- 11-Witchcraft, psychic, mediumship, and paranormal ultimate techniques.

All are based upon the Kira'at (Readings) and Dirasaat (Study) of the Enlightened Masters Ulema.

The present book (Volume III) introduces and outlines some of the major topics and exercises of Cadari-Rou'yaa, Chabariduri, and Fik'r-Telemetry, (called psychometry in the Western world) the seeker of enlightenment learns in the third and fourth years at the Mystic Ulema Ma'ahad.

The actual curriculum is much extensive and complicated. Nevertheless, we have selected for you, important concepts, Kira'at and Dirasaat that the Western mind could understand to a certain degree.

Preface

The techniques, methods, art and science of remote viewing, locating and finding objects and missing persons, gathering information about people, objects and places just by looking at photographs of objects, people and places, and by sensing the vibrations emanated from photographs and objects, and in many instances by touching objects and photographs, are grouped into the Mystic Ulema Ilmu (Learning) under three secret esoteric techniques known as:
- 1-Cadari-Rou'yaa
- 2-Chabariduri
- 3-Fik'r-Telemetry, called psychometry in the Western world.

These techniques were shrouded in secrecy for almost 5,000 years. They were developed by the Mystic Anunnaki Ulema Jamiya in the Near East, and some 3,000 years ago, the priests of Ra and Melkart began to implement them in Egypt, Sumeria and Phoenicia.
The Babylonian and the Chaldeans were famous for their practice of these esoteric techniques, and some of the techniques and exercises were explained at length in the Book of Ramadosh.

Cadari-Rou'yaa, Chabariduri, and Fik'r were discussed in depth in several previous published work of Maximillien de Lafayette. But they are herewith introduced to the readers and the lightworkers as part of the curriculum and training/orientation programs of the American Federation of Certified Psychics and Mediums.

*** *** ***

Terminology/Glossary of Technical Terms

Araya: The net or web of the mind. The Araya contains multiple Jabas, each one has a specific function. All Jabas all linked to each other through a web. Negative Jabas eliminate productivity and imagination. Araya can be strengthened though the Supersymetric Mind exercise.

Cadari: A grid; a plasma-screen.

Fik.Ra.Sa: The ability of reading others' thoughts.
The Arabic word "Firasa" is derived from Fik.Ra.Sa. In Arabic, it means the ability to read thoughts, to understand the psyche of a person just by looking at him/her.

Fik'r: The primordial source of life for our physical body. Some have depicted it as the primordial source of energy that makes the body function and maintain its equilibrium.

Fik'r-Telemetry: One of the advanced techniques used to identify the nature and origin of an object, as well as, the mental, etheric and physical properties, character, profile and identity of a person, just by touching the object or the photo of that person

Firasa: A technique which is still used in Arabic today and refers to reading others' intentions, thought, and mind in general. It applies aloso to reading their thoughts and intentions at distance; another form of mental remote viewing.

Iama: The 4 levels of the mind:
1-Level one: Tabi'a.
2-Level two: Irtifa.
3-Level three: Tanra.
4-Level four: Kamala.

Iama: A technique which was used in ancient times by the seers of Chaldea, sages of Persia and the Arab Peninsula. In that part of the world, Iama was known as Firasa.

Ira'ha: The mind's state of neutrality.

Irtifa: The second level of the mind.

Jaba: Every thought, each idea you have in your brain, has a vibration. And each vibration occupies a spot in your Araya, called "Jaba".
Let's simply things and call Araya now a net.
This net has many holes, called "Jabas". Each Jaba (A hole, so to speak) stores one idea. And each idea or thought in the Jaba of the net produces a vibration.
For example, if the net has 70,000 Jabas, your brain will be able to store 70,000 ideas and thoughts. This means, that your Araya hosts 70,000 vibrations. And that is full capacity. Some people who are more creative than you could have 300,000 ideas and thoughts stored in 300,000 Jabas (Holes or locations) in your Araya (Net).
The good thoughts and good ideas in your Araya do not expand. They stay well balanced and well synchronized where they are (Inside the Jaba of the net). There, they are safe and protected. Only bad thoughts, and bad ideas, such as fear, low self-esteem, stubbornness, hate, indecisiveness, laziness, tendency toward violence, badmouthing people, envy, jealousy, betrayal, so on, emit vibrations that overflow the perimeter (Circumference) of the Jaba (Hole or location) that stores your thought or idea. This phenomenon (Overflow) takes over the adjacent Jaba(s) containing a good idea or a good thought.
Because the negative energy inside your mind is usually stronger than the positive energy of a good thought, the Jaba on the net (Location) containing a good thought or a good/positive idea shrinks, gets contaminated, and stops to emit positive and creative energy.
This, kills the good thoughts and good ideas in your Araya. If this continues, all good and creative ideas and thoughts in your brain will be damaged and neutralized by your bad thoughts and ideas.
This will stop your creativity. In other words, many cells in your brain's or Araya's, and their creative mental faculties stored in the Jaba become dysfunctional; atrophied or dead. In this case, you are responsible for causing this deterioration.
Nobody has forced you to think about bad thoughts or bad ideas. It is your own doing. You might say, I have no control over all this.

Things happen. Ideas come and go.
And I will tell you, you are wrong, because you can control your ideas and your thoughts, and make them work for you in a very healthy, positive and productive way.
The most destructive thoughts that prevent you from succeeding in life are:
- a-Low self-esteem;
- b-Fear (Fear of anything);
- c-Unwillingness to accept new ideas;
- d-Bitterness;
- e-Constantly contradicting others because you have developed a complex of inferiority, and not because of a complex of superiority;
- f-Negativity.

Note: a to f are not categorically part of the Anunnaki's primordial (Original) makeup of the genetic creation of your mind. Your upbringing, way or life, and personal vision of the world and your immediate environment could have caused this.

Kamala: The fourth level of the mind.
It represents enlightenment, a perfect harmony with the Micro and the Macro, and the mastery of supernatural powers.
The Ulema described it as the final stage/level of complete awareness, and unification/unity with the ultimate state of Oneness.

Khateyn Tarika: Every human being on Earth is lined up with two invisible lines that determine her or his balance (Equilibrium) and a synchronized harmony with their immediate surroundings, as well as the size and strength of his or her luck in this physical world. These two lines are called Khateyn Tarika.
They exist around our body, and are lined up in a parallel manner. They could reach a length of 6 feet. They serve as a protection shield. If you are "Outside Khateyn Tarika", you will never reach the top, in anything you do, no matter how happy, intelligent, influential, and rich you are."
The Sahiriin and Rouhaniyiin told us that every human being on Earth is lined up with two invisible lines that determine her/his balance and harmony with their immediate surroundings, as well as the size and strength of his/her luck in this physical world.

Khateyn means: Two Lines. It is the plural of Khat, which means one line. They are invisible to the naked eye. The Rouhaniyiin nicknamed Khateyn "Tarik al Hayat", meaning the road of life.
These two lines determine how healthy, successful and balanced you are or will be in your life.
Tarika means a path, a road.
It is usually linked to your present and future, with major impact on your health, love life and business. Khateyn Tarika is directly linked to your "Double", astral body, your mind, spirits and entities who live here on Earth, and in other dimensions.
All of us, big and small, lucky and unlucky, rich and poor, famous, infamous and unknown, are conditioned and influenced by Khateyn Tarika two invisible lines that exist either ahead of our body, behind it, or around it.
And the position and placement of these two lines that we cannot see –unless we were taught how to find them– have a major impact on everything we do, and think about. Khateyn Tarika technique will positively influence or change your life, health and luck. Khateyn Tarika is one of the most important, mind-bending and powerful parts of Ilmu (Knowledge and wisdom), and the secret doctrine of the Allamah and Rouhaniyiin. If you unlock its secrets, you will reach your full potential, and accomplish the impossible. Khateyn Tarika will put you on the right track, leading to spectacular success, power, awareness, and harmony with your environment, and perfect health.
Note: I wrote a booklet on Khateyn Tarika, please refer to it. Master Khafaja Sudki Ghayali said verbatim: "If you are "Outside Khateyn Tarika", you will never reach the top, in anything you do, no matter how happy, intelligent, powerful, influential, and rich you are."

Kira'at: Ulema readings.

Ma bira-rach: The etheric image of your brain (Mind).

Ma'aad "Ma'had": School or center of learning of the mystic Ulema.

Makan-Zaman: A connection between a place and events to occur.

Maska: The healing touch.

Mounawariin: The enlightened Ulema, the Illuminated teachers; one of the 4 categories of the Ulema Anunnaki. It derived from the word Nour, which means light.

Nizraat Takaroob: Nizraat means vision, and Takaroob means, getting closer. The general meaning is to bring things together, and/or to merge them together.
Nizraat Takaroob is a mental/spiritual exercise aimed at developing mental images and extra-mental faculty that partially activate the Supersymetric Mind.

Rou'yaa: A vision, a perception.

Rouhaniyiin: A noble title given to the medieval and some contemporary alchemists and Kabalists. Seers who deal with noble spirits. Seers and Masters who practice the art and science of Arwaah (Spiritism).

Sahiriin: Plural of Saher (magician or sorcerer).
Saher derived from the Pre-Islamic Arabic word Sihr, which means sorcery and magic.

Supersymetric Mind (SM): According to the theory of supersymetry, also known as SUSY, all particles in the known universe have their counter-part, also called super-partner(s).
Basically, this is the view of quantum physics scientists and theorists. In the Anunnaki-Ulema context, supersymetry is either the similar or the opposite of you.
In a limited sense, it is the other super-partner of "you", and what constitutes you at all levels; organically, bio-organically, chemically, genetically, etherically, atomically, mentally and physically. The most important and predominant part of your mind-body supersymetry is your mind. Because everything starts in your mind. In this context, your mind is a "Supersymetric Mind". You were brought up to believe that every person in the world has a brain; one single brain.
Nobody seems to contradict this. And I do not contradict this either. However, this "single brain" is not the only brain you have, at least in this dimension.
All of us, enlightened or not have two brains; the first brain is the one we are aware of, and familiar with, from studying anatomy, medicine and other disciplines, and the other mind, is the one

that co-existed, and currently co-exists side-by-side your brain, and outside your body.

Tabi'a: The first level of the mind.

Takaroob: Basically and essentially what we do via the practice of Takaroob is entering the mind of another person, picking up one idea or one thought at the time, and transposing it to the grid of our mind, thus, the other aspect of our mind (Brain) called "Supersymetric" could read it.
The word Firasa is still used in Arabic today and refers to reading others' intentions, thought, and mind in general. It applies aloso to reading their thoughts and intentions at distance; another form of mental remote viewing.

Tanra: The third level of the mind.

Tarik: Road. Usually used as "Tarik al Hayat", meaning the road of life, and sometimes, the path of luck, as written in the book of fates and destinies. Tarik exists inside Khateyn Tarika, the two invisible lines that border the human body, and condition our state of mind.

*** *** ***

Chapter I
Cadari-Rou'yaa Technique
Reading the thoughts, intentions and feelings of others

Definition:
Cadari-Rou'yaa is the Ulemite name or the term for a secret technique developed by the mystic Anunnaki Ulema, and Mouwariin (Enlightened Masters) centuries ago, that enabled them to read the thoughts, intentions and feelings of others, either by visual observation and/or by sensing the vibrations of objects and people. It is also used in remote viewing, locating missing persons and objects, and applying the Maska, which is the healing touch.
It is composed of two words:
a-Cadari, which means a grid; a plasma-screen.
b-Rou'yaa, which means vision; perception.

Cadari-Rou'yaa is also a method to diagnose health and prevent medical problems from occurring in the present and future, by reading and interpreting the rays and radiations, a human body diffuses on a regular basis. In the West, it is called reading of the aura.
The following is an excerpt from an Ulema's Kira'at (Reading) I heard and studied at the Ma'aad (Ma'had) some 55 years ago. It is herewith reproduced verbatim (Unedited), from a Kira'at, as it was given by an Anunnaki-Ulema in the Middle East.
Ulema Sadiq is talking to his students (Verbatim):

The Technique:

- **1**-You are going to learn wonderful things today. But you have to remember that you should stay calm, focused and relaxed all the time.

- **2**-You are going to succeed. But you should not give up too easily. Don't get frustrated and despaired because it is not working right away. At the beginning, everything needs additional effort, a great deal of patience and a strong belief in yourself.

- **3**-We are not asking you to have a blind faith. Leave faith to others. Use your mind instead. Follow the procedures. Practice, practice, and practice. And everything is going to be just fine.

- **4**-I repeat this one more time. Don't get frustrated and anxious if it is not working right away. It is going to work and your patience will pay off.

- **5**-Now, go to a quite place. We suggest your private office if you are sure nobody is going to interrupt your practice, or just your bedroom if you can be by yourself, alone, quite and distant from noises.

- **6**-You have to practice alone. Always alone.

- **7**-Good. Take a piece of paper. A plain sheet of white paper with no lines. Size: 7 centimeters by 6 centimeters.

- **8**-On the left side of the paper, draw a red circle. Size: 2 centimeters in diameter.

- **9**-Next to the red circle, and at a distance of 1 centimeter, draw a small black dot. Size: Half the size of a bean.

- **10**-Next to the black dot, and at 1 centimeter distance, draw a green circle. Size: 2 centimeters in diameter. The color of the circle could change later on. And you will understand why. It could happen at the time you focus is well-anchored.

- **11**-All should be aligned equally and straight on the same line. (Same level)

- **12**-Now you have from left to right: A red circle, a black dot, and a green circle, all on the same line.

- **13**-Make sure the sheet of paper is placed 25 centimeters in front of you. It is very important that you keep this distance.

- **14**-Close your eyes for 4 seconds or so.

- **15**-Open your eyes, and breathe slowly and deeply.

- **16**-Close your eyes one more time for 2 seconds.

- **17**-Open our eyes, and breathe one more time slowly and deeply.

- **18**-Now, look straight at the black dot for just 2 seconds or so.

- **19**-Close your eyes for 2 seconds or so.

- **20**-Open your eyes now, and look one more time at the black dot for 40 seconds or so. Remain patient and focused.

- **21**-Now, tell your left eye to look at the red circle and your right eye to look at the green circle at the same time.

- **22**-I know it is strange and seems confusing to you. But don't worry.

- **23**-Try again.

- **24**-Keep on trying until you get it right.

- **25**-Now, something unusual is going to happen. Pay attention.

- **26**-You will start to see both circles getting closer.

- **27**-It is not an optical illusion.

- **28**-On the contrary, it is an optical adjustment, because now, your eyes and your mind are working together. Something you have not done before.

- **29**-Now, something very new and very unusual is going to happen.

- **30**-Keep looking at those circles.

- **31**-Do not loose concentration.

- **32**-Watch now what is going to happen. A new shape is going to emerge. A new color is going to appear.

- **33**-The blue circle on your left starts to look very different. It has something around it. Something you did not see before.

- **34**-The blue circle has some sort of a lighter color ring around it. It could be any color. It does not matter.

- **35**-Remember you are still looking at both circles at the same time.

- **36**-Don't leave one circle to go to another circle.

- **37**-Now, the green circle on your right starts to look very different. The green circle has now something around it. Something you did not see before. Pay attention to the color's variation.

- **38**-The green circle has some sort of a lighter color ring around it. It could be any color. It does not matter.

- **39**-Remember you are still looking at both circles at the same time.

- **40**-Don't leave one circle to go to another circle.

- **41**-Keep looking at both circles for two minutes or so.

- **42**-Something unexpected is going to happen now. Pay attention to the motion of the black dot.

- **43**-It would/could appear to you that the black dot is moving somehow.

- **44**-Don't let this distract you.

- **45**-Anyway, it will go away in a few seconds.

- **46**-Something very important is going to happen now. Pay attention.

- **47**-The ring around the blue circle on your left is getting bigger and denser.

- **48**-The ring around the green circle on your right is getting bigger and denser.

- **49**-And you are still looking at both circles.

- **50**-You are doing absolutely great.

- **51**-Now, focus your attention on the blue circle on your left.

- **52**-Something very important is going to happen now. Pay attention.

- **53**-The longer you look at the blue circle, the stronger and brighter the ring around it becomes.

- **54**-Now the ring around the blue circle is getting denser. Pay attention to new intensity of the color of the ring.

- **55**-In less than 2 seconds, the ring becomes much, much brighter and starts to radiate.

- **56**-Now move to the green circle on your right.

- **57**-Focus your attention on the green circle on your right.

- **58**-Something very important is going to happen now. Pay attention.

- **59**-The longer you look at the green circle, the stronger and brighter is the ring around it.

- **60**-Now, the ring around the blue circle is getting denser.

- **61**-In less than 2 seconds, the ring becomes much, much brighter and starts to radiate.

- **62**-You are seeing now something you have never seen before. And, that is good.

- **63**-Breathe deeply and take a short brake. (One minutes)

- **64**-Repeat the whole exercise from the very top.

- **65**-This should do it for now.

- **66**-Tomorrow, you will practice again.

- **67**-You will do the same thing.

- **68**-Keep on practicing like this for 5 consecutive days.

- **69**-If it did not work, do not give up.

- **70**-Be patient. It will work. It did work for many students.

- **71**-It is simply a matter or practice, perseverance and patience.

- **72**-And hopefully, if it did work, the rings you saw around the circles were the vibrating auras of the circles.

Note: According to the Ulema, this exercise opens an extra visual/optic dimension for your eyes and your mind. In fact, it did not open anything new; it has just activated your visual perception.
You had it all the time, but you were not aware of it.

*** *** ***

Chapter II
Chabariduri Technique

Learning From Sensing the Vibrations of Objects and People at Distance

---

Definition:
Chabariduri is the name of an Anunnaki-Ulema technique and exercise to develop the faculty of remote viewing, thus enabling you to find, locate and see objects and people at distance.
The Anunnaki Ulema taught their students the art and science of remote viewing to improve their knowledge, enrich their awareness, and widen their perception of life, and not to spy on others, as it is the case in the West. Chabariduri can also be used to see and assess objects and people aura, vibes and energy at distance.
Chabariduri is also known as Fik'r-Telemetry; it is one of the advanced techniques used to identify the nature and origin of an object, as well as, the mental, etheric and physical properties, character, profile and identity of a person, just by touching the object or the photo of that person. I wrote about this subject in several books, and especially in "How to Use Your Mind Power to do the Impossible: Esoteric techniques to activate the mental power of your mind."
In this section, I will be summarizing some of the most important concepts and preliminary instructions to read and/or to find/locate a person or an object just by looking at a photo.
You have to remember that everything around you, including all life-forms and objects have some sort of energy, and a multitude of vibrations, including the photos you will be looking at.
By sensing the vibes emanated from the photographs you are looking at, you should be able to create a fair assessment of what you are seeing, such as, identifying the object, the location of areas/places, the character and psyche of people you see in the photographs, and so on.

Herewith a synopsis of one of the mystic Ulema remote viewing techniques.

Mystic Ulema Kiraat:
Note: The Ulema hand over to each student two small stones of the same size.

Stage One:

- **1**-Pick up any stone you want and write on it Aleph "A" (First letter in many Semitic and ancient Middle/Near Eastern languages).

- **2**-Squeeze on the stone and try to feel something, anything or try to think about something, anything you want.

- **3**-Put the Aleph stone on your desk or on a solid surface.

- **4**-Pick up the second stone and write on it Beth "B".

- **5**-Squeeze strongly on the stone.

- 6-Try to feel something, anything, or try to think about something, anything you want.

- **7**-Put the Beth stone on your desk or on a solid surface.

- **8**-Write down on a white paper what did you feel or what did you think when you touched stone Aleph.

- **9**-Draw a line and write below the line what did you feel or what did you think when you touched stone Beth.

*** *** ***

Stage Two

- **10**-Now, use another sheet of paper.

- **11**-Take stone Aleph and put it in your right palm. Close your hand. Close your eyes.

- **12**-Breathe slowly and deeply. Squeeze on the stone and ask yourself where did the stone come from. Ask yourself this question 4 times.

- **13**-Put down the stone on your desk. Open your eyes. Take the pen and start writing on the paper what you are thinking about. It does not matter what. Just write down what your mind is telling you.

- **14**-Now try to guess where did the stone come from.

- **15**-Try to associate the stone with places you know and places you don't know.

- **16**-Draw on the paper whatever you see in your mind.

- **17**-Think strongly. You may close your eyes if you want.

- **18**-You still have 2 minutes to finish the test.

Stage Three

Note:
Now, the Ulema tell the students time is up.
One of the students is asked to collect the papers and to deposit them on the desk of the Ulema.
After having reviewed the students' answers, the Ulema direct those who passed the test to move to a designated area in the classroom. The master dismisses those who failed. If all the students failed the test, the session comes to an end and another test will resume the following day.
Now, the students are asked to do the same thing with stone "Beth." Same instructions are given, and same procedures are followed. Those who pass the test stay in the classroom and those who failed are dismissed.

From my Kira'at at the Ma'aad:
Note: Talking to my students and adepts who have successfully passed the test). From my Kira'at at the Ma'aad:

- **1**-Now you are going to work with stone Aleph. Stone Beth is no longer needed.

- **2**-Now you are going to describe the place where the stone came from. You are going to write down everything you see or think of.

- **3**-You will write down on a new sheet of paper anything you will be thinking about, anything and everything, no matter how silly or unrealistic it appears.

- **4**-Do not hesitate. Do not doubt yourself. Don't wait to have a second thought.

- **5**-Rush your visions, thoughts and feelings to the paper.

- **6**-Now hold the stone in your right hand and squeeze on the stone firmly for one minute.

- **7**-Put the stone down and start writing.

- **8**-Write down your first thoughts.

- **9**-If you start to feel or think that you already know something or anything about the place where the stone might have come from, write down the name and location of the place right away.

- **10**-Do not hesitate. You should not doubt yourself. Hesitation will immediately interrupt the smooth flow of extra-visual perception.

- **11**-Follow your instinct, follow your thoughts, follow your feelings, follow your vision and stop there. Meaning you stop and you start focusing on the place you have reached or imagined in your mind.

- **12**-Tell your mind that you that you are already there; you are looking mentally at the place you have reached or seen in your mind. If you manage to convince your mind that you are looking mentally at the place you have reached, a cell in your brain called "Conduit" will trigger images and visions that could create and temporarily produce multiple mental-physical projection of objects, things, people, houses, shops, gardens, children, trees, water, bicycles, cars, buildings, streets, animals…many, many things or maybe just a few things. It doesn't matter how much you see, or what you are seeing at that moment. Let your "Conduit" do the trick. Write down everything you saw, as much as possible.

- **13**-Now, make a list of what you have seen. Do not follow any particular order. Of course, many visions will jump at you, and don't try to arrange them and list them on the paper according to priorities and importance. Go with the flow of your Conduit.

- **14**-Describe what you have seen. Meaning, once you have listed all the visions and images' projections, describe in one or two lines, each image you saw in your mind. In some cases, I recommend that you draw an illustration of the images you saw. This will anchor in your mind, various depictions of the object or image you saw.

- **15**-Be precise; give as much details as you can and name things…be specific about colors, sizes, forms, shapes, dimensions, locations…anything around, below and above the items you see.

- **16**-You don't need to follow any particular order in listing what you see. First, write down everything you see, later we will sort them out together.

- **17**-Now draw a large square on the paper, and in the center of the square, try to connect all the images to the place you have reached. For instance, if you have seen windows, bridges, buildings, streets, trees, so on; list the mental images in sequences.

- **18**-Start first with the buildings, followed by the windows, continue with streets, bridges, trees, etc. This listing will create what the Ulema call "Conduit logic" which has nothing to do with traditional mental logic. But it will help your mind to create a sequence of "Makan-Zaman", which means connection between a place and events to occur.

- **19**-In doing so, you are transposing and transporting your mind to a different time-space continuum. You will not succeed in your remote viewing exercise as long as your mind is retained by the location you are in, and the time you are spending on your remote viewing. For example, if you are doing your exercise in your room in New York City, you should tell your mind that you are no longer in New York City. And if you are conducting your remote viewing exercise at 7:00 PM, you should tell your mind that the time is no longer 7:00 PM. In doing so, you free your mind from the limitation and frontiers of your time-space. You have to escape your time-space in order to enter another time-space dimension, which stores the information you are searching for. It is not difficult to accomplish this, if you keep telling your mind that you are no longer in New York, and the time is no longer 7:00 PM. Again, your Conduit has a logic (Called Meta-Logic) that your mind does not have in normal situations.

- **20**-You don't have to make a masterpiece in drawing the images' projections. Small sketches are fine; any kind of sketches. Even small icons, a few lines here and there, even a series of lines and geometrical forms will suffice for now; draw anything you see or think you are seeing.

- **21**-Do not attempt to force yourself to give any explanation to what you are seeing or drawing. You will think about it, later on.

- **22**-Now, concentrate on the place you have found and write down everything you see...draw more pictures...do not delete anything...keep adding but don't delete.

- **23**-What you put on paper, what you draw, and what you write down are exactly what your mind has perceived; it is an accurate projection of the object or the person you sought.

- **24**-By applying the Ulema Fik'r-Telemetry technique (Described on the following pages), you will be able to gather enough information about all the images you saw during your initial remote viewing exercise.

*** *** ***

Fik'r-Telemetry: Ulema Psychometry

I. Definition and introduction:
Fik'r-Telemetry is one of the Chabariduri's advanced techniques used to identify the nature and origin of an object, as well as, the mental, etheric and physical properties, character, profile and identity of a person, just by touching the object or the photo of that person.

II. Objectives and purposes of these exercises:
Remember, everything around you in the world, including life-forms and objects have some sort of energy, and a multitude of vibrations, including the photos you will be looking at, in this chapter.
By sensing the vibes emanated from the photographs you are looking at, you should be able to create a fair assessment of what you are looking at, such as, identifying the object, the location of areas/places, the character/psyche of people you see in the photographs, and so on. Try to remember what you have already learned from previous exercises. Apply your learning to all the photos in this chapter.

You are going to identify a few things:
a- Objects:
You will be asked to look at the photos of various types of objects, ranging from cars and slabs to commercial products and documents.

You are required to identify the object, its origin, properties, etc., just by touching the photo with your right or left palm. And in some instances, you will be asked to tell if you feel good or bad about these objects, meaning if you feel good vibes or bad vibes coming from the objects you are looking at, and just by touching the photographs.

b- Areas and places:
You will be asked to look at the photos of various installations, buildings, edifices, areas, and places. And in some instances, you will be asked to tell if you feel good or bad about these areas and places, meaning if you feel good vibes or bad vibes coming from the places and areas you are looking at, and just by touching their photographs with your right or left palm.
You are required to identify the location of these areas and places, just by touching the photo with your right or left palm.

c- People:
You will be asked to look at the photos of people from around the world, ranging from leaders and artists to celebrities and obscure or unknown people.
You are required to identify those people, and in some instances, you will be asked to tell if you feel good or bad about them, meaning if you feel good vibes or bad vibes coming from the people you are looking at, and just by touching their photographs with your right or left palm.

III. The Exercise:

Note: These mental-esoteric exercises are not techniques, but simply exercises to test your psychic abilities, and to find out whether you have or have not learned and/or developed psychic, mental, esoteric, and spiritual faculties. However, I will provide you with brief instructions to guide you on the right path. You should concentrate by visually focusing on the photo. Do not guess!
Try to sense vibrations or anything unusual just by touching the photograph.

Generalities/Basic Steps
The mental-metaphysical process

_____

Follow these instructions:

- 1-First thing to do is to gaze at the center of the photograph for 5 seconds.

- 2-Now, very slowly look at the upper left side of the photograph for approximately 10 seconds.

- 3-Very slowly look at the right side of the photograph for approximately 10 seconds.

- 4-This will give you a global visual perception of the photograph.

- 5-Take a deep breath.

- 6-Close your eyes for approximately 5 seconds.

- 7-Open your eyes now, lean forward toward the photograph, and place your right or left palm on the photograph.

- 8-Close your eyes for approximately 10 seconds, and try to not think about anything.

- 9-Mentally, create inside your mind an absolute state of tranquility.

- 10-You can accomplish this, by visualizing in front of you a rainbow of a multitude of colors, while your eyes are closed.

- 11-If it is difficult to visualize the rainbow, place your left hand above your head, press on the photo with your right palm, and take a deep breath.

- 12-Open your eyes, drop down your left hand, and press on the photograph with your right palm.

- 13-If you are left-handed, do just the opposite.

- 14-Hold the photograph in your left hand, and press again on the photograph with your right palm.

- 15-Run/move your right palm over the photograph in a circular motion, starting from left to right.

- 16-Keep doing this for 10 seconds.

- 17-Now do the opposite; move your right palm in a circular motion, from right to left for 10 seconds.

- 18-Stop, and concentrate intensely on the photograph.

- 19-Pull back a little bit. Allow the photograph to breath and send you its vibes.

Looking at the photograph of an object
- 20. If you are looking at the photograph of an object, try to see it as a negative slide. See Illustration below.

Illustration #1 Object

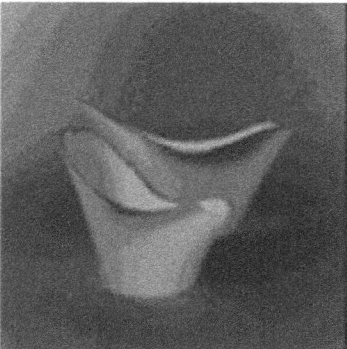

Original picture   The negative slide

- 21. Create a space in your mind or in your imagination for Illustration #2 Object. See illustration below.

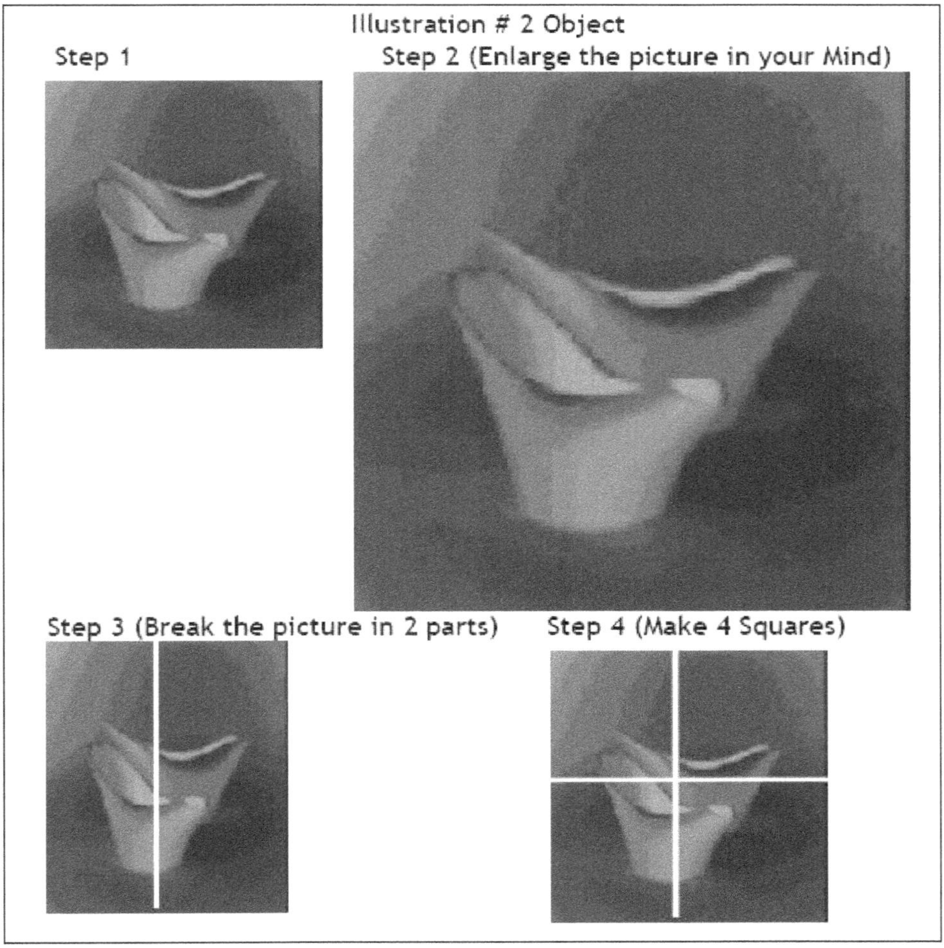

Illustration # 2 Object
Step 1
Step 2 (Enlarge the picture in your Mind)
Step 3 (Break the picture in 2 parts)
Step 4 (Make 4 Squares)

- 22. Drag the negative slide to the left (Step One).

- 23. Enlarge the negative slide as shown in Step 2, and place it on the right side of the place you have created in your mind or imagination.

- 24. Divide the picture in 2 parts, as shown in Step 3, and place it on the left side of the place you have created in your mind or imagination.

- 25. Divide the picture in 4 parts, as shown in Step 4, and place it on the right side of the place you have created in your mind or imagination.

- 26. Have a kook at Illustration #3 on the next pages.

- 27. Keep in your mind the picture listed under Step 1.

- 28. Mentally create a blank square in the center of the picture, as seen under Step 2.

- 29. Mentally enlarge the picture which has the blank square, as seen under Step 3.

*** *** ***

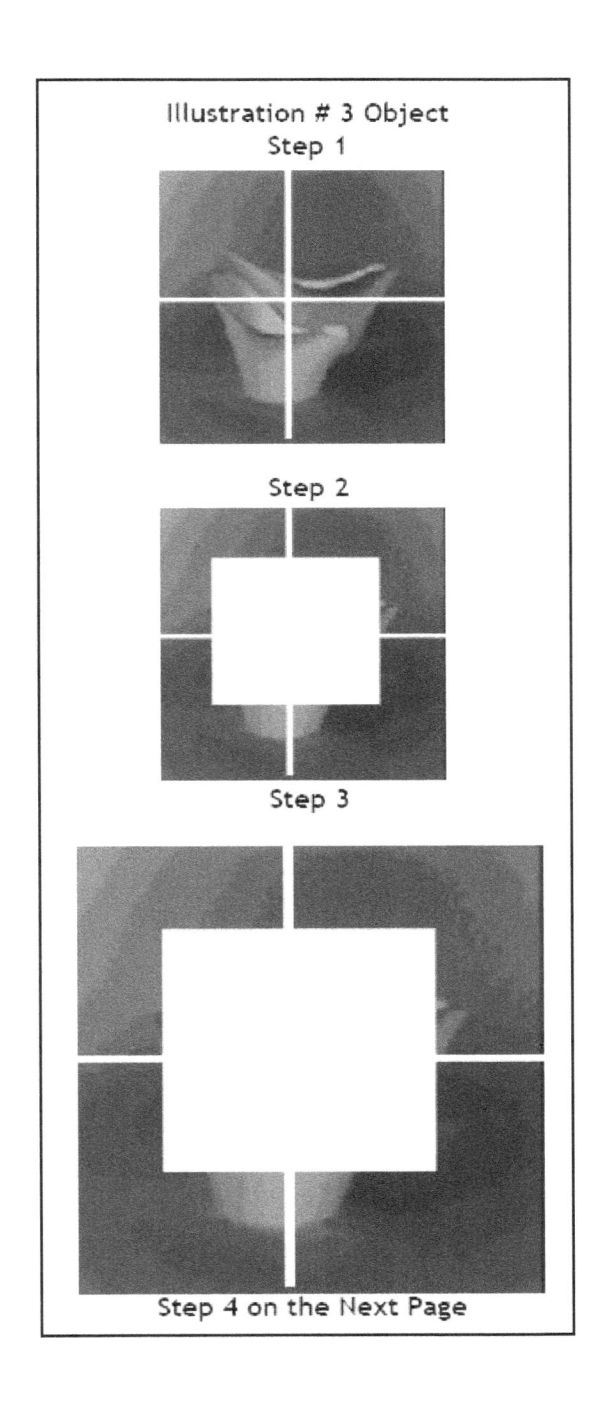

Illustration # 3 Object
Step 1

Step 2

Step 3

Step 4 on the Next Page

- 30. Place the original photograph of the object inside the blank square.

- 31. Concentrate on the photograph of the object inside the blank square.

- 32. Let your mind for a few moments anchor itself in the blank square.

- 33. When your mind is ready, meaning ready to send you a message, you will feel a new kind of sensations (Vibrations) coming your way, more precisely toward your forehead.

- 34. As soon as the vibrations hit your forehead, you will be able to read very clearly the message of your mind who has analyzed these vibrations.

- 35. And the message will include vital information about the nature, origin and location of the object.

- 36. This is a new discovery you have made, that you will never forget as long as you live, because you have entered the un-chartered world of mind transmission, and remote viewing using your Mind and vibrations you caught from looking at or touching an object.

This technique will also help you locate lost objects, such as keys, rings, jewelry, documents, a wallet; any object you were looking for. And if you need additional guidance, do not hesitate to write to me.

*** *** ***

Illustration # 4 Object

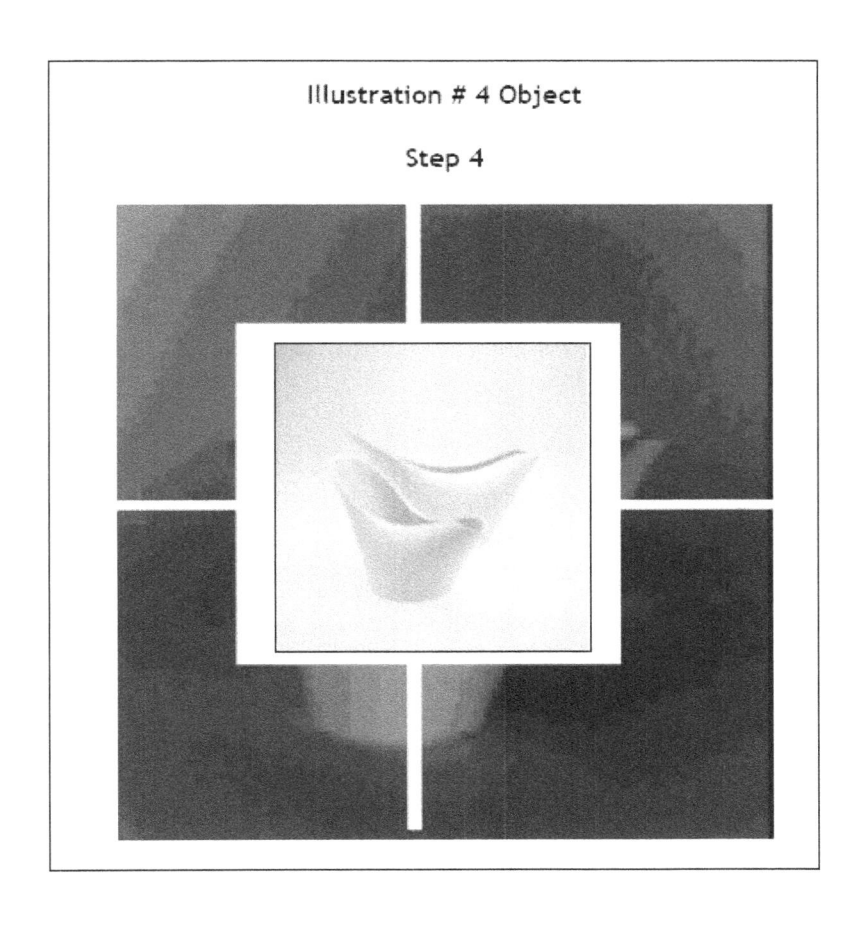

Step 4

Looking at the photograph of a person.

Note: If you follow my instructions, and you do it right, you will be able not only to identify the person in the picture, but also to discover lots of things about him or her, including character, habits, temperament, level of spirituality and intelligence, thoughts and intentions stored inside his or her Khateyn Tarika, and even locate that person.
You will believe it when you see results, and you will get result when you learn the technique, so start working on it. If you need more help, write to me.

*** *** ***

Follow these instructions.

Phase One:

- 1-All photographs emit vibrations, thus, you will be able to feel vibrations coming from the photograph of the person you are looking at.

- 2-Hold the photograph in your left hand for 20 seconds, and press on the photograph with your right palm for 20 seconds.

- 3-If you are left-handed, do just the opposite.

- 4-Place the photograph on a solid surface, your desk or a regular table are just fine.

- 5-Look at the upper left side of the photo for 5 seconds, then look at the upper right side of the photo for 5 seconds.

- 6-Take it easy, relax, easy does it. It is going to work like a charm. I am with you all the way.

- 7-Let the photo sit on the solid surface for 5 seconds or so, this will allow the photograph to anchor some of its vibes into the solid surface.

- 8-Pick up the photograph and place it upside down on the solid surface for 5 seconds.

- 9-Pick up the photograph, place it back on the solid surface, and rotate it clockwise.

*** *** ***

Phase Two:

- 10-Pick up the photograph, make now a copy of the photograph, and reduce its size by approximately 55 to 60%.

- 11-Place the original photograph on the left side of the solid surface, and the copy on the right side, as shown in Illustration #2 Person, (Step 1 and Step 2).

- 12-Superpose the reduced photograph in the center of the copy of the photograph, as shown in the illustration (Step 3) and place on the left side of the solid surface, right below the original photograph.

- 13-Let this arrangement of photos sit on the solid surface for 5 seconds.

*** *** ***

Illustration #2 Person

Step 1: The Original photograph

Step 2: Copy of the photograph

Step 3: Superpose the reduced photo

Phase Three:

- 14-Look at Illustration #3 Person on this page.

- 15-Re-arrange the photos as seen in the illustration.

- 16-In your mind, link the 3 photos together, meaning creating a three dimensional representation.

- 17-You can do this by telling yourself that the photo on left represents time zone, the photo on the right represents space/location zone, and the photo in the center represents a sphere/level where you will retrieve information about that person.

- 18-Have a look at Illustration #4 on the next pages.

Phase Four:

- 19. Now you must concentrate on the photo shown in Illustration #4 Person, on the page.

- 20-Place your right or left palm on the top of the photo, for 10 seconds.

- 21-Take a deep breath.

- 22-Let your mind for a few moments anchor itself into the photo.

- 23-When your mind is ready, meaning ready to send you a message, you will feel a new kind of sensations (Vibrations) coming your way, more precisely toward your forehead

- 24-Ask your mind to respond to the questions listed under the photo of a person (They are several in the book) published in this book.

- 25-For example, on pages to follow, the questions are: Is this person a good person? Did he serve well his community or just the opposite? On another page, the questions are: Is this person a good person? Was she a great civil right activist? And how did she die? So on.

- 26-As soon as the vibrations hit your forehead, you will be able to read very clearly the message of your mind who has analyzed these vibrations.

- 27-And the message will include vital information about the person in the photograph, as well as answers to the questions you have asked.

Illustration #4 Person

NOTE

For reasons I can't disclose, I am not in a liberty to teach you right now, techniques related to find military areas and locations of places. Thank you for your kindness and understanding

***   ***   ***

Chapter III

Your Ulema psychometry and remote viewing tests start here in this chapter

Faces of People
Objects
Places
Products
Artwork

*** *** ***

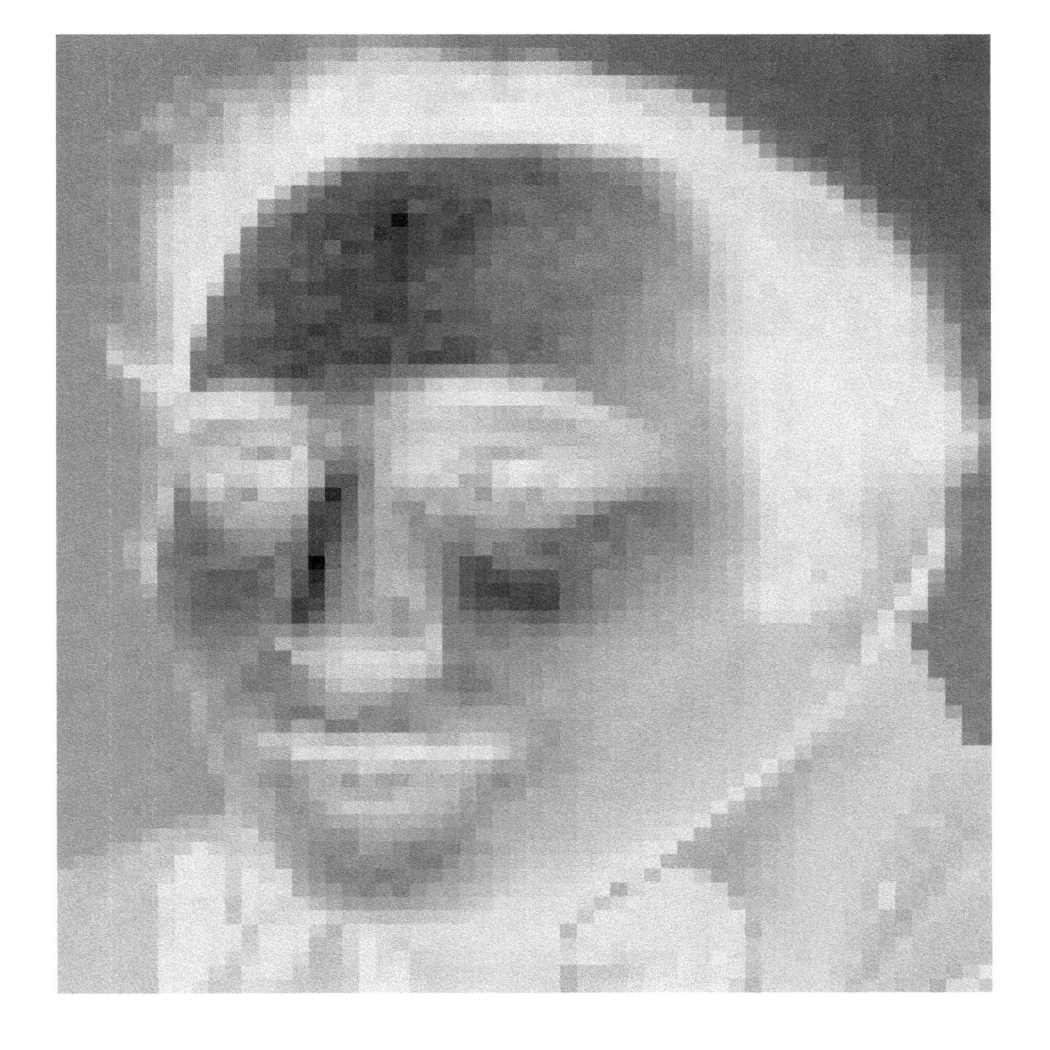

YOUR TESTS START HERE WITH THIS PAGE

DON'T TURN THIS PAGE YET, OR YOU WILL SPOIL EVERYTHING!!

Reply to the questions, using the previously mentioned techniques:

Is this person a good person? Did he serve well his community or just the opposite?

This is a pixelized and negative photo of a person who, a few years ago made headlines. On the next page, you will see the normal picture. If you have already recognized the person in the negative picture, do not continue this exercise.

55

The photograph belongs to serial killer David Berkowitz, a.k.a. Son of Sam. So, the correct answer to the question becomes obvious.

DON'T TURN THIS PAGE YET, OR YOU WILL SPOIL EVERYTHING!!

Reply to the questions, using the previously mentioned techniques:
Is this person a good person?
Was she a great civil right activist? And how did she die?

This is a pixelized photo of a person who made headlines. On the next page, you will see her normal picture. If you have already recognized this lady, do not continue this exercise.
Find the correct answers on the next page.

57

This photo belongs to Teresa Lewis, 41, who died by injection in Virginia. "Lewis enticed two men through sex, cash and a promised cut in an insurance policy to shoot her husband, Julian Clifton Lewis Jr., and his son, Charles." Source: AP.

DON'T TURN THIS PAGE YET, OR YOU WILL SPOIL EVERYTHING!!
Reply to the questions, using the previously mentioned techniques:
Who is this person?
How did this person die? Select one answer.
Answer #1. Car accident.
Answer # 2. He was assassinated.
Answer #3: Old age.
Answer # 4: Blood transfusion.
The correct answer is on the next page.

This photo belongs to Mohandas Karamchand, known as Mahatma Gandhi (1869 – 1948). He was assassinated on January 30th 1948.

DON'T TURN THIS PAGE YET, OR YOU WILL SPOIL EVERYTHING!!
Reply to the question, using the previously mentioned techniques:
Can you identify this place? The correct answer is on the next page.

This is the photograph of an abandoned Russian military base.

DON'T TURN THIS PAGE YET, OR YOU WILL SPOIL EVERYTHING!!

Reply to the questions, using the previously mentioned techniques:
Anything special about this young woman?
Can you identify her?
The correct answer is on the next page.

Left: This is the picture of a young Mother Theresa, at the age of 18. Right: Mother Theresa, how we remember her.

DON'T TURN THIS PAGE YET, OR YOU WILL SPOIL EVERYTHING!!

Reply to the question, using the previously mentioned techniques:
What is or was the profession of this person?
If you have recognized him, disregard this test.
The correct answer is on the next page.

This is the photograph of the legendary French Cubist painter, Georges Braque.

DON'T TURN THIS PAGE YET, OR YOU WILL SPOIL EVERYTHING!!

Reply to the question, using the previously mentioned techniques:
What is the profession of this person?
The correct answer is on the next page.

This is the photo of the multi-talented Alain Chabat, a French actor and director.

DON'T TURN THIS PAGE YET, OR YOU WILL SPOIL EVERYTHING!!

Reply to the questions, using the previously mentioned techniques:
Can you identify this place? Where this slab is located?
A nearby area will suffice.
The correct answer is on the next page.

This slab is located nearby Flagstaff, in Arizona, USA.

DON'T TURN THIS PAGE YET, OR YOU WILL SPOIL EVERYTHING!!

Reply to the question, using the previously mentioned techniques:
What this person does for a living?
The correct answer is on the next page.

He is a politician.
This is the picture of Canadian Senator Romeo Dallaire.

DON'T TURN THIS PAGE YET, OR YOU WILL SPOIL EVERYTHING!!

Reply to the question, using the previously mentioned techniques:
Is this person a spy, a prisoner of war, or a gay activist?
The correct answer is on the next page.

This is the picture of former Russian spy Alexander Litvinenko.

DON'T TURN THIS PAGE YET, OR YOU WILL SPOIL EVERYTHING!!

Reply to the question, using the previously mentioned techniques:
Who from these two stars committed suicide?
If you have already recognized any of them, disregard this test.
The correct answer is on the next page.

Carole Landis, the lady on the left, committed suicide in 1948, in her home, in Pacific Palisades, California, by taking an overdose of Seconal. She was 29 years old.

DON'T TURN THIS PAGE YET, OR YOU WILL SPOIL EVERYTHING!!

Reply to the questions, using the previously mentioned techniques:
Can you identify this document?
Who wrote it?
The correct answer is on the next page.

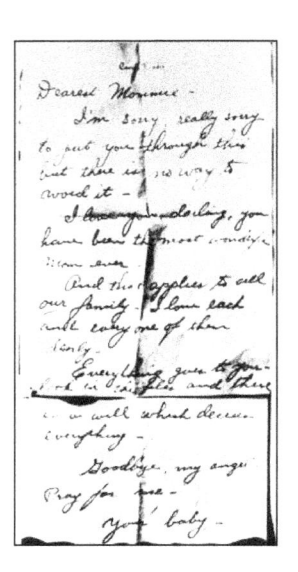

This is the suicide/farewell note of actress Carole Landis, to her mother Clara.

It reads: "Dearest Mommie: "I am sorry, really sorry, to put you through this. But there is no way to avoid it.

I love you Darling. You have been the most wonderful mom ever. And that applies to all our family. I love each and every one of them dearly.

Everything goes to you. Look in the files, and there is a will which decrees everything.

Good bye, my angel.

Pray for me.

your baby."

DON'T TURN THIS PAGE YET, OR YOU WILL SPOIL EVERYTHING!!

Reply to the questions, using the previously mentioned techniques:
Was/is this a successful product?
What kind of vibrations do you feel by looking at this product or by touching it?
The correct answer is on the next page.

This product is very successful.
You should get good vibes from touching it.

DON'T TURN THIS PAGE YET, OR YOU WILL SPOIL EVERYTHING!!

Reply to the question, using the previously mentioned techniques:
Was/is this a successful product?
What kind of vibrations do you feel by looking at this product or by touching it?
The correct answer is on the next page.

Can of Bambeanos; a product that did not do well in 1974-1975. It was an early soybean snack by Colgate-Palmolive.

DON'T TURN THIS PAGE YET, OR YOU WILL SPOIL EVERYTHING!!

Reply to the questions, using the previously mentioned techniques:
Was this car a very successful or a failed model?
What kind of vibrations do you feel by looking at this picture or by touching it?
The correct answer is on the next page.

This is Edsel car, which was manufactured by Ford in 1958. It was a total failure in the United States.

DON'T TURN THIS PAGE YET, OR YOU WILL SPOIL EVERYTHING!!

Reply to the question, using the previously mentioned techniques:
Which painting is real, and which painting is fake?
The correct answer is on the next page.

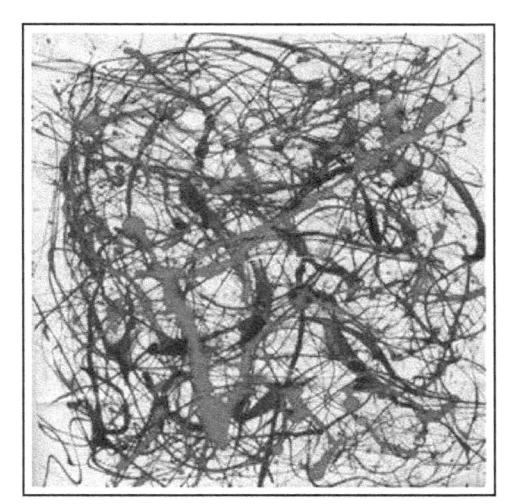

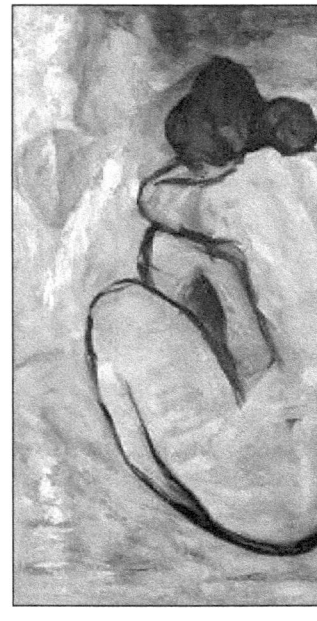

Both painting are fake.

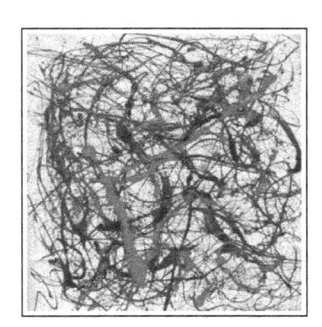

The one on the top is an imitation of a real painting by Jackson Pollock.

The one below is a forgery of a painting by Pablo Picasso, executed by Michael Zabrin.

Chapter 4
Your First Reading

Note: Reading a woman's vibes is different from reading a man's vibes, and you will find out why on your own. If you have already assimilated what you have read and practiced on the mystic Ulema and Mounawariin's techniques I described in the book, you will be able to read people's vibes and see their aura.

However, the instructions provided in this chapter will guide you step-by-step toward implementing what you have learned so far, even though, you might think that what you have read didn't tell you much on how to see people aura and learn about their psyche and character.

Let's set-up the scene:

Place: A cocktail party, a reception, an exhibition, a social gathering, etc.
Time: Irrelevant, for you can read people vibes at any time.
You have been introduced to a person (A man). You follow the etiquette rules and you stand where you are. Be polite but do not show emotions.
First thing to do is to remain calm and don't move much. Stay within the perimeter of a person's Khateyn Tarika, and follow these instructions.

Reading the face of a person

Instructions:
1-You must stay calm but you should think fast, meaning you have to remember right away what you have learned from the techniques I described in the book.
For instance, item #8 from Cadari-Rou'yaa Technique is to be considered and applied right away: "On the left side of the paper, draw a red circle."

The left side here is one foot to 2 feet at the right side of the person you are looking at. The red circle is an image you create in your mind.

2-In your mind, draw a small black dot, and insert it in the imaginary red circle. (Note: This was item #9 from Cadari-Rou'yaa Technique.)

3-Move the red circle and anchor it on the face of the person you are looking at, for 1 second.

4-Bring the red circle to his chest, and anchor it there for 1 second.

5-Drop down the circle to his abdomen area and anchor it for 1 second.

6-Let the circle now flow over his knees down to his feet.
This should take less than 2 seconds.

7-What you have done so far is Scanning his body.
The scanning took less than 5 seconds. By Ulema standard it is too long. The Ulema can scan a human body in less than 2 seconds. And The Ulema Mounawiriin in a second.
But it is OK now, because you are a beginner.

8-While the circle is scanning the person's body do not move your head up and down. Very discreetly, let your eyes follow the movement of the circle. In the future, you will be able to follow the scanning without looking at what the circle is doing.

9-Now the scanning is done, what's next? The circle on its own will go up and position itself on the whole body of the person you are looking at.
Meaning what?
Well, the circle will get bigger and bigger until it absorbs the whole body of the person.
The circle becomes the etheric zone of the physical body.
In other words, the circle is now the Aura of the person.
Surprise? Yes! A lovely surprise indeed.

10-As the circle gets bigger and bigger, it changes colors.
(Note: This was item #10 from Cadari-Rou'yaa Technique.)

11-Changing colors means that the body of the person you are looking at is reacting to something, it could be you or to some other things he is feeling or thinking about.
His reaction will display a certain color corresponding to his state of mind, as well as emotional moods.
Colors vary in intensity and shades according to what the person is going through, thinking about and feeling.

12-In order to accomplish this, tell your left eye to look at the red circle and your right eye to look at the dot which now is green. (Note: This was item #21 from Cadari-Rou'yaa Technique.) In the future and as you progress in your study, your Fik'r will take care of what your both eyes are doing.

13-When the circle and the dot become one, you will begin to see the true color(s) of each of his thoughts, feelings, and intentions. (Note: This was item #26 from Cadari-Rou'yaa Technique.)

14-Each part of his body emits a defined color. In your first reading, you will be a little bit confused because you don't know what to do with all these colors coming from everywhere, how to sort them, how to categorize them, and how to assess them, all simultaneously.
But in the future you will be able to do so at ease.
It is a matter of practice.

15-To make it easy on yourself, focus on the face of the person you are looking at.
Don't bother with colors jumping at you right and left, up and down. Just concentrate on his face.

16-At the very beginning, his face will emit one color.
This is the "initial" color, meaning what he is feeling right now. The color refers you to his state of mind at this very particular moment, but most certainly the "initial" color is about to change to other colors.
And the change means that his mood is changing; he is thinking now about something else, he is reacting to you and to what you are saying; he is up to something.
Well, let's find out what he is up to?

But before we do that, we must analyze his "initial" color, because it reveals the true state of mind and the emotional mood of the person at the time you met him.
In other words, the "initial" color is a projection of his true "Self". Add to the fact, that the sudden change of the "initial" color to other colors will help you see and understand his New state of mind and his New emotional mood, including but not limited to his dispositions, intentions toward you, and whether he is sincere or playing games with you, whether he is telling you the truth or lying, whether he is truly friendly or just the opposite.

17-Analyzing the "initial" color:
a-If you see orange or yellow colors: The person is OK. He has a good nature, or at least he is in a good mood.
These are called "Good Colors".
b-If you see black, grey, or pale beige colors: Something is wrong with this fellow.
Perhaps his health condition, financial problems, worries, or simply his current emotional mood.
These are called "Bad Colors".

18-The most important phase of reading the person's vibes and seeing his aura takes place when pertinent colors begin to change when you are looking at him, because they are either influenced by your presence or by the way he feels towards you, and what he is up to.
(Note: This was item #32 from Cadari-Rou'yaa Technique.)
And this is your chance to find out if he is OK, or a person to avoid.

19-Changes in colors: If the "initial" color changes to gray or black, the change indicates that person is not sincere; he could be lying to you, hiding something that could hurt you in the present or the future, or simply he is trying to camouflage himself. In other words, he is not the person who he pretends to be; he is deceitful.
If the "initial" color remains the same, this is an indication that the person is honest and truthful. If the "initial" color changes to red and dark blue, this is an indication that the person has a bad temper; he could be violent and very abusive. Sudden changes in colors usually occur as a result of or a spontaneous reaction to numerous things, such as:

- a-A discussion you are having with this person,
- b-A political opinion,
- c-A business proposal,
- d-Expressing a feeling,
- e-An offer of any sort,
- f-A sexual desire, etc.

Of course, this reading is solely limited to the face of the person.
But I have to remind you that reading the vibes and seeing the aura in order to size up and penetrate a person's real character should not be your only satisfaction, for if the bad colors get intense, they could cause you –in certain conditions and situations– harm and disrupt the smooth rhythm of your own aura and Khateyn Tarika, including damages to your computer, electronic equipments, and even the serenity of your own place.
People bad vibes negatively affect you and suck up your mind and body energy. Henceforth you must right away protect yourself by using the protection shield "Hatani".

Seeing the aura and reading the vibes centered around the chest.

The vibes and rays centered around the chest and the abdomen refer to the health condition of a person. The Anunnaki Ulema told us that an accurate diagnosis of health conditions could be done by looking at the energy vibes emanated from the region of the solar plexus and the abdomen. More on this in Book 4.
If you need any additional guidance and instructions on any of the subjects and techniques mentioned in the book, do not hesitate to contact me at delafayette6@aol.com

*** *** ***

Chapter 5

Reading Peoples' Thoughts Via Iama Technique

I. Definition:
The Iama technique was used in ancient times by the seers of Chaldea, sages of Persia and the Arab Peninsula. In that part of the world, Iama was known as Firasa.
The word Firasa is still used in Arabic today and refers to reading others' intentions, thought, and mind in general. It applies aloso to reading their thoughts and intentions at distance; another form of mental remote viewing.

In Ana'kh literature, Iama is usually depicted as a triangle representing four levels of the mind:
- 1-Level one: Tabi'a.
- 2-Level two: Irtifa.
- 3-Level three: Tanra.
- 4-Level four: Kamala.

I have explained this concept in my book "Activation of the Conduit and the Supersymetric Mind."
The Supersymetric Mind (SM) plays a paramount role in the mode of operation of Iama. Once your SM is activated via the "Nizraat Takaroob Technique", you will become able to read others' mind by transposing their thoughts, one at the time, from one part of your mental grid to another. I have also explained the Takaroob technique on pages 68-93 in the book previously mentioned.
Basically and essentially what we do via the practice of Takaroob is entering the mind of another person, picking up one idea or one thought at the time, and transposing it to the grid of our mind, so the other aspect of our mind called "Supersymetric" could read it.

The Takaroob technique is unrelated to reading the aura and the body's energy diffused through colors; it is purely mental.

The Anunnaki Ulema and the Mounawariin told us that the mind as a grid, like the Cosmos has its net, fabric, web.
All sorts of ideas and thoughts circulate over the grid, like light and cosmic rays circulate over the landscape of the universe.
Henceforth, the ideas and thoughts circulating over the mental grid of another person could be caught by your mind and transmitted to your own mental grid.
At first, it seems confusing and unrealistic to you. But in reality and in pragmatic application it is a simple mental (Telemetric Though Projection) exercise if you know the Takaroob technique. In this chapter I will reproduce the illustrations of the mental grid and the "Nizraat Takaroob Technique"; the integral explanation of its mode operation is found in the book "Activation of the Conduit and the Supersymetric Mind."

Let's simplify things.
The basic idea is this: Each house has its own foundation. The universe (Space of the Cosmos) has its own "Fabric", it is the fabric of time-space and space-time. And the mind has its own "Grid"; a large flat surface upon which all sorts of ideas and thoughts float. You position yourself (Your mind) outside or above the grid of others' mind, and you observe their ideas and thoughts floating.
How do you position yourself above or outside others' grid?
Well, I am going to give you a synopsis of this technique. And later on, I will explain to you step-by-step how to catch others' thoughts (One idea, one thought at the time), transpose it to your mind's grid, read it, and find the truth about them.

II. Synopsis of the technique:
The synopsis is demonstrated via illustrations on the following pages.

Generalities:
The grid represents the surface that contains the whole spectrum of others' thoughts. The triangle represents one single thought.
Transposing the position of each triangle will mentally lead to "transporting" others' thoughts to another triangle that's belongs to your own mind. See illustrations (Grids and triangles) and explanations on the following pages.

III. How to use the Nizraat Takaroob technique:
Follow these instructions.

Illustration #1:
Step #1. You start concentrating on this screen (Grid). Meaning, try to identify the two different positions of the triangles.

Illustration #1: The Grid

IV. Identifying the two positions of the triangles of the Grid

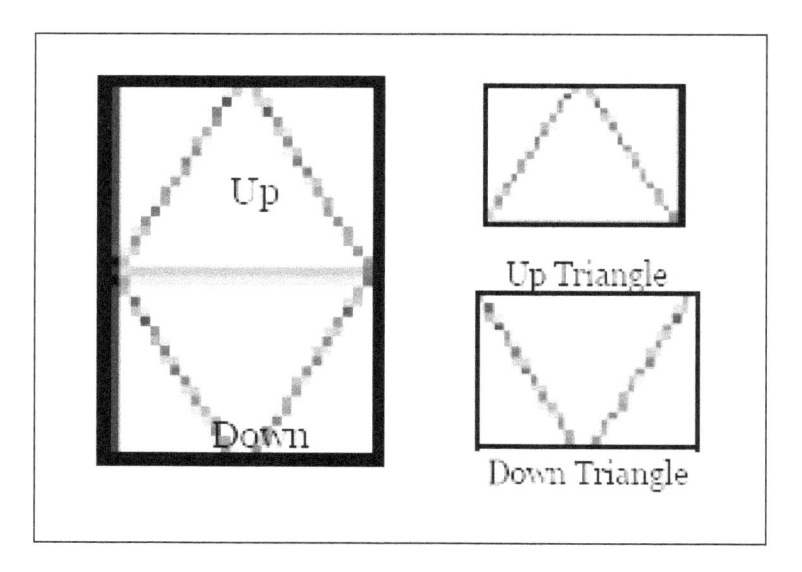

Step #2. Tell your mind that each triangle represent one though (Others' thought).
Thus, the Grid has hundreds of thoughts.
- Look for more triangles.
- Keep identifying more triangles:
- "Up Triangles", and
- "Down Triangles".
- Spend approximately 2 minutes on this exercise. This will anchor you into the grid. Do not ask why, just do it.

Important note: While you are doing this, keep telling your mind that each triangle represents one thought (Others' thought).

Step #3. Now, try to identify the "Double Triangles"; one Up, and one Down. Spend approximately 2 minutes on this exercise.

*** *** ***

Illustration of a "Double Triangle".

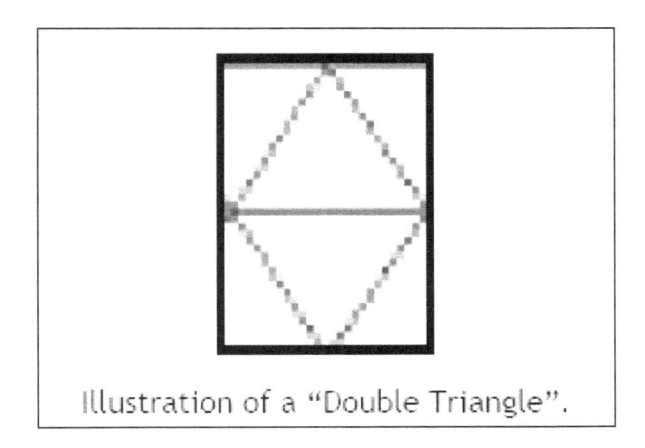

Important note: While you are doing this, keep telling your mind that each triangle represents one thought (Others' thought)

***   ***   ***

Reading peoples' thoughts

Nizraat Takaroob Technique
Illustration #1: In your mind place these 2 triangles on the Grid.

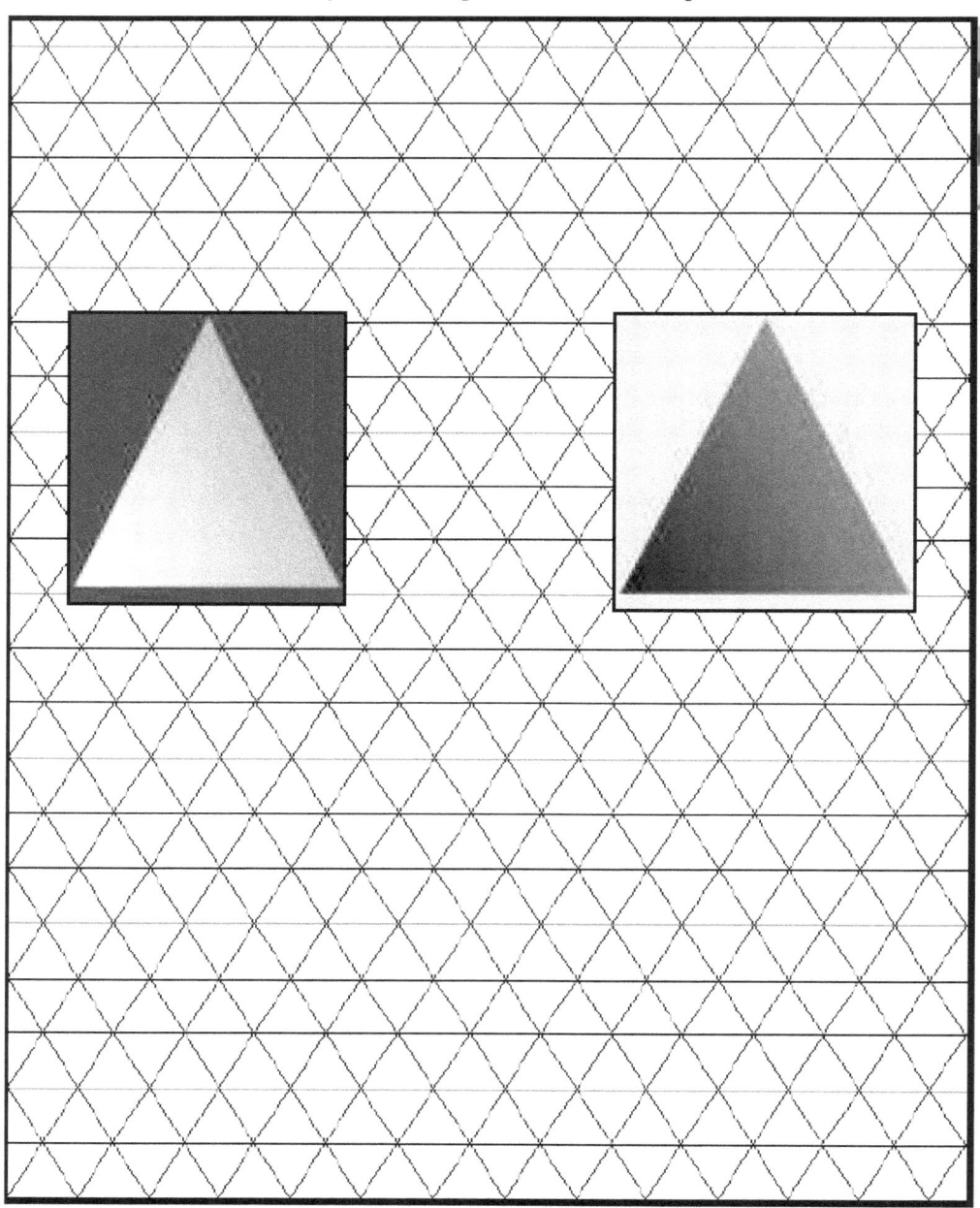

Write on this page how many "Up Triangles", "Down Triangles", and "Double Triangles", you have identified so far.
Example:
20 Up
15 Down
10 Double

You write here:
Up:_____

Down:_____

Double:_____

***   ***   ***

Reading peoples' thoughts

Step #4: Now concentrate on the left triangle you have previously placed on the Grid (see the triangle below) for approximately 5 seconds.

Left triangle

Step #5: Now concentrate on the right triangle you have previously placed on the Grid (see triangle below) for approximately 5 seconds.

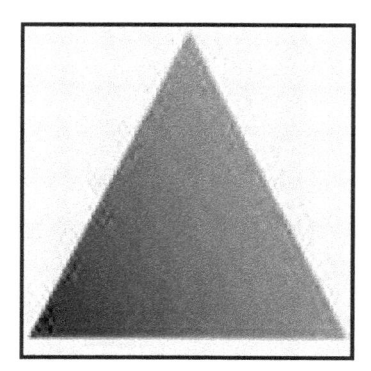

Right triangle

Important note: While you are doing this, keep telling your mind that each triangle represents one thought (Others' thought)

Step #6: Now, look at the right triangle and the left triangle simultaneously (at the same time).

Step #7: Tell you mind that you want to bring the right triangle closer to the left triangle.

Step #8: You can do that if you concentrate on the very top of the right triangle for ten minutes.
Focus on this part of the triangle.
See below:

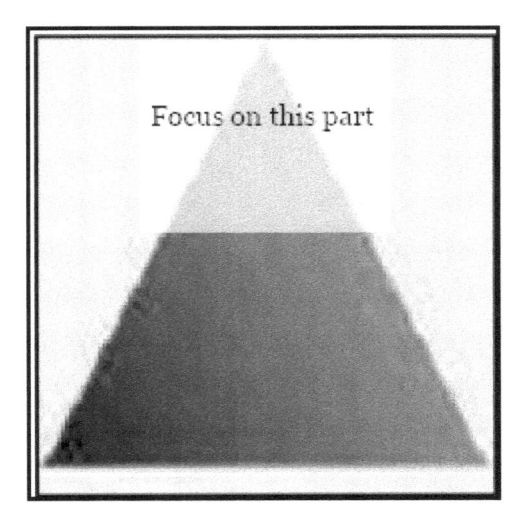

Important note: While you are doing this, keep telling your mind that each triangle represents one thought (Others' thought)

Step #9: Look at illustration #2, on the next pages.
You should get the result, as seen on the next pages.
If you succeed in doing this, then what you are seeing is not a hallucination, but a Mental Transposition of an object, from one place to another. You will absolutely succeed with practice, patience, and perseverance.

Do not underestimate the power of your mind. Once this phase (Step#9) is accomplished successfully, your Supersymetric Mind will be partially activated.

Expect to fail in your first and second attempts. Nothing wrong with that. You are entering an un-chartered zone of the mind. But eventually, you will succeed!

Important note: While you are doing this, keep telling your mind that each triangle represents one thought (Others' thought)

Reading peoples' thoughts
_____

Illustration # 2

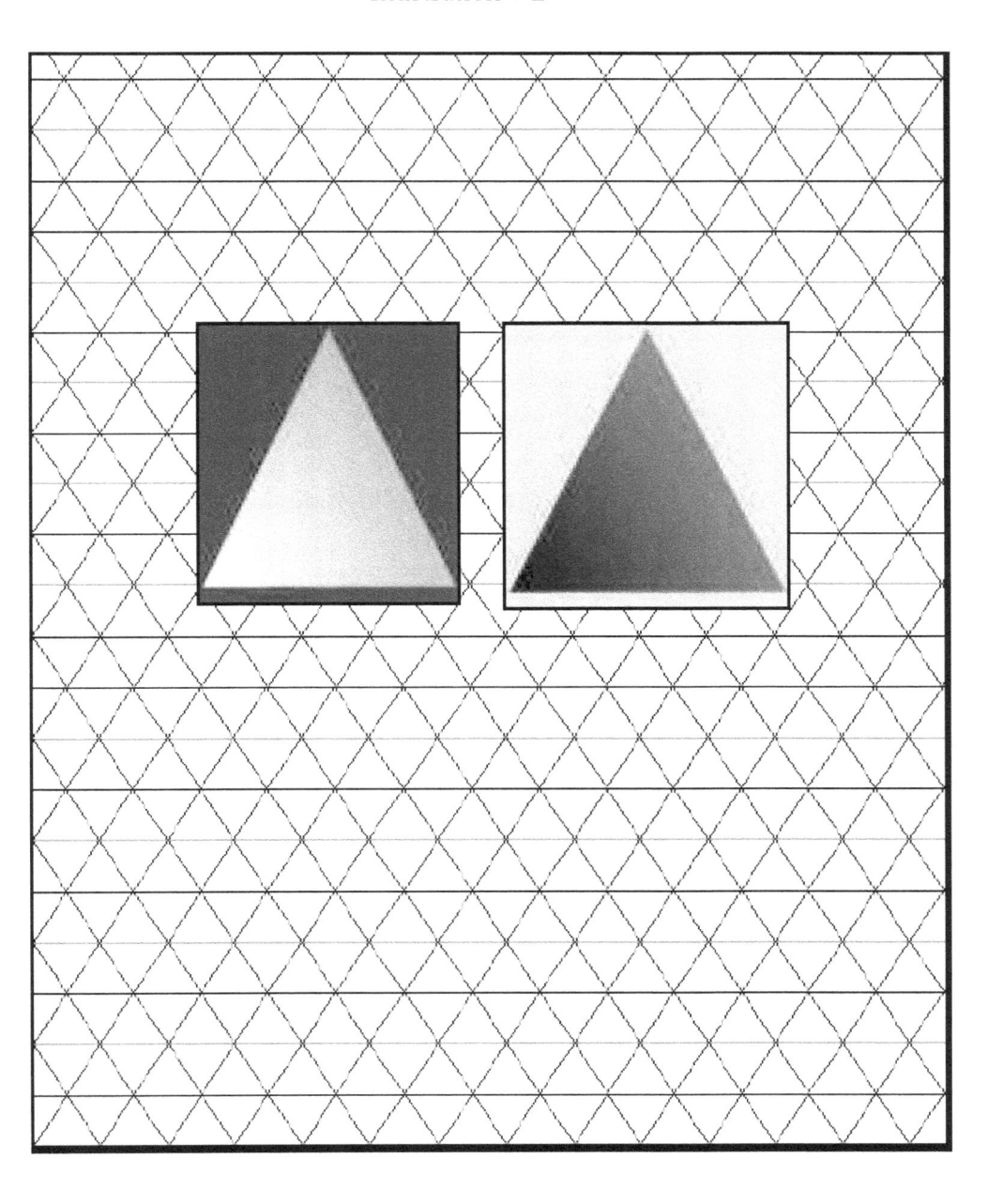

Additional instruction:
If you have failed more than 3 times, do this:

- a-Tell your mind that the top of the triangle (Square in shade) is much lighter in weight than the base of triangle.
- b-Focus on the top of the triangle for 5 minutes or so.
- c-Command the top of the triangle to lift up and separate itself from the whole triangle.
- Keep repeating this command mentally for 2 minutes.
- d-You are going to be amazed by the result of your deep concentration. The top will separate itself from the whole triangle, and will come closer to the left triangle. It is going to happen. No doubt about it.
- e-As soon as the top is close to the left triangle, the whole triangle will shift itself toward the left triangle.
- See illustration #2.

Important note: While you are doing this, keep telling your mind that each triangle represents one thought (Others' thought)

Step #10: Mentally command the right triangle to merge with the left triangle. See illustration on the next pages (Illustration #3). On the following pages, I will explain to you how you can do it.

Important note: While you are doing this, keep telling your mind that each triangle represents one thought (Others' thought)

Reading peoples' thoughts

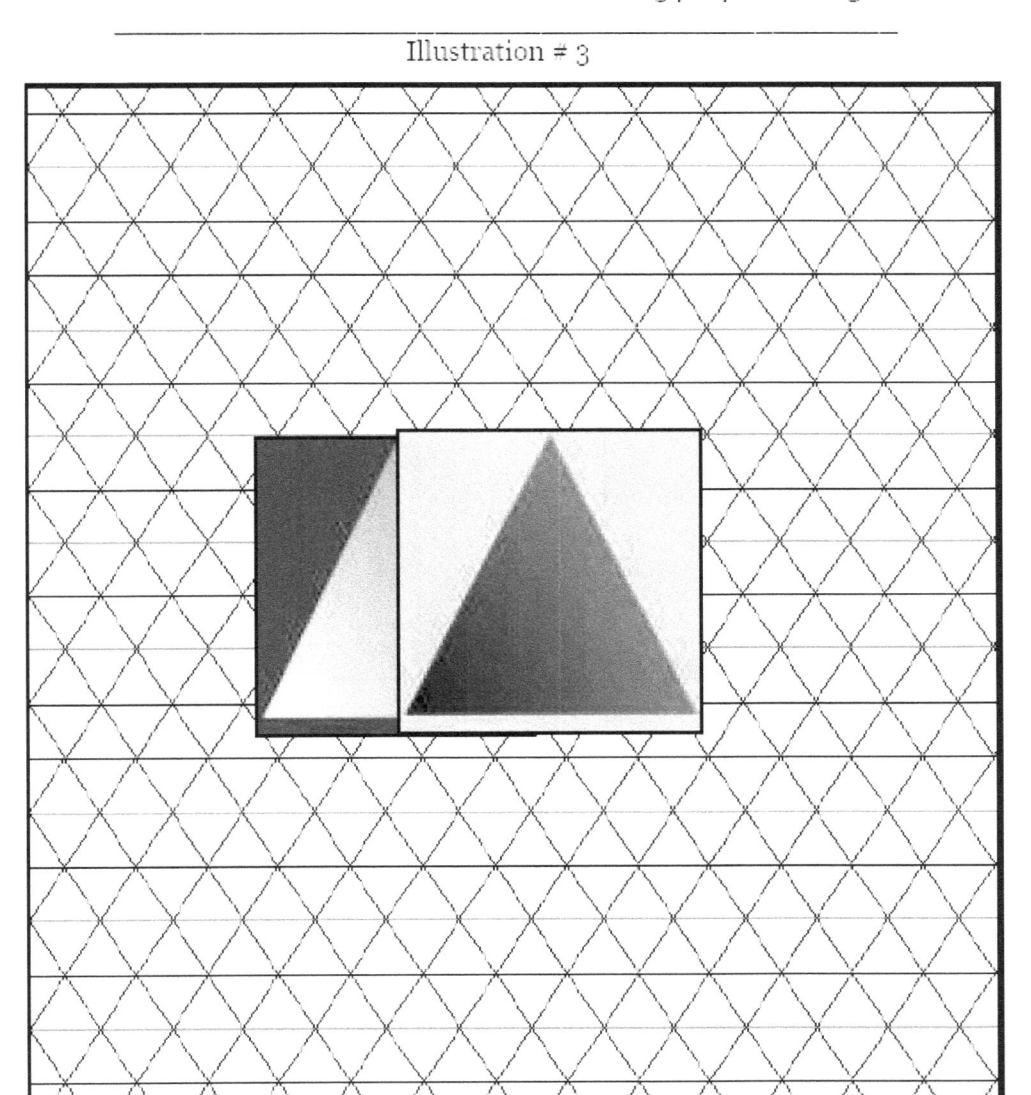

Illustration # 3

105

Reading peoples' thoughts

Instruction for step #10:

a- Look one more time at the illustration #3 (Previous page.)
This is how the 2 triangles merge.

Merging of the 2 triangles.

Important note: While you are doing this, keep telling your mind that each triangle represents one thought (Others' thought)

***   ***   ***

106

b- Although, you are still using your "regular" mind, and no Supersymetric Mind has yet manifested itself, do not be concerned with this. It is activated to a certain degree. Don't tell yourself, well, I am not using this Symetric thing, where is it? It is only a mind game.
Don't ever say that.
Once you are fully anchored into the grid, and your mind starts to get busy with the right triangle, the left triangle, the Up triangle, the Down triangle, moving one triangle closer to another one, so on...once all these activities are being progressed, and while you are still focusing on all these mental exercises, your Supersymetric Mind will kick off, out of the blue. It will take over.
Your "regular" mind will be pushed aside temporarily, your mental visualization will increase considerably, and suddenly your Supersymetric mind begins to guide you in your experiment/exercise. How this is done? You will find out, later, and on your own, and no further explanation is needed.
Please, keep telling yourself: "I can do it! I can do it! I can do it!" You have to believe in yourself, and in the power of your mind. Don't give up too fast and too easily.

Important note: While you are doing this, keep telling your mind that each triangle represents one thought (Others' thought)

All the students of the Anunnaki Ulema practiced the Nizraat Takaroob, and all succeeded in activating their Supersymetric Mind. Practice makes perfect!
Esoteric studies and mental development are not easy to understand, simply because there is no physical and realistic explanation that could make you understand what is happening here. If others have succeeded in these exercises, why shouldn't you join the club?

c- If the right triangle is not getting closer to the left triangle, or not close enough, close your eyes for 5 seconds, and direct your attention to the base of the left triangle.

d- Focus on the lower base of the left triangle.
See illustration on the next page.

***   ***   ***

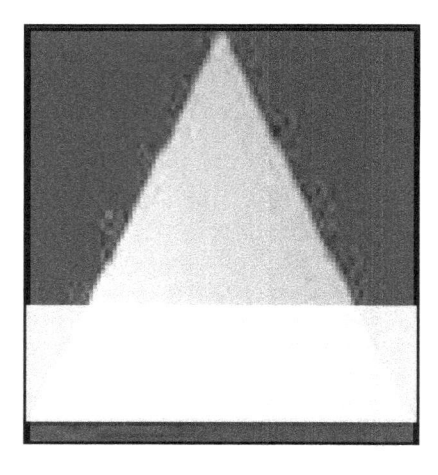

Base of the triangle

---

e-And now, fast, and back and forth, and without stopping, move your eyes from the base of the left triangle to the top of the right triangle, and vice versa...Don't STOP!! Keep doing this for 10 seconds, and Voila! Both triangles are merging now almost perfectly! It wouldn't take more than 9 seconds!
You did it. Congratulations!!
To see the result, look at illustration #4.

***   ***   ***

Reading peoples' thoughts

Illustration # 4

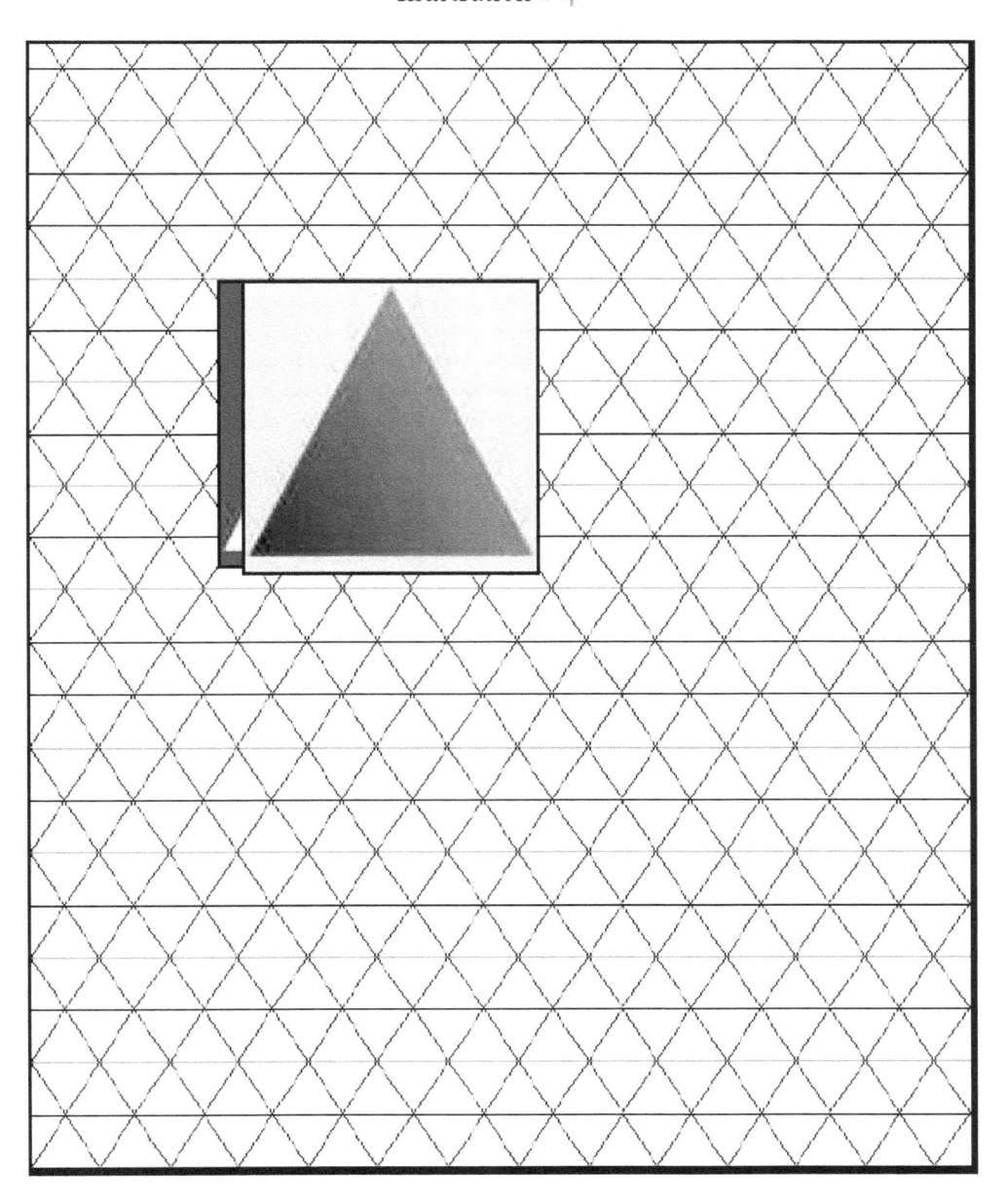

Reading peoples' thoughts

Step #11: Look at the illustration #5.
Now you are going to reverse the whole process. Meaning, you are going to do just the opposite. I will explain:

Look at these 2 triangles that we took from illustration #5.

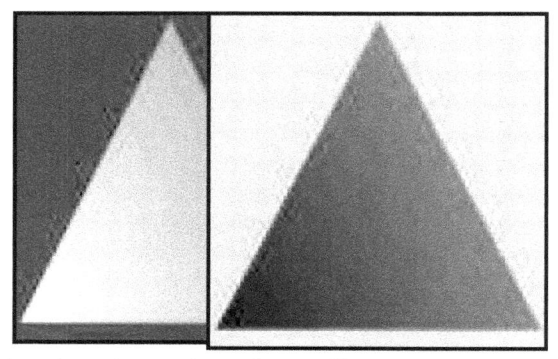

2 triangles taken from illustration #5.

Important note: While you are doing this, keep telling your mind that each triangle represents one thought (Others' thought)

***   ***   ***

110

By now, you have partially activated your Supersymetric Mind. Your "regular" mind is dormant, and that's wonderful. Reversing the whole process, and pushing aside the right triangle is a piece of cake.
Why?
Because your very powerful Supersymetric Mind is in charge now. It is going to require a minimal effort and a very short time to accomplish this.

Step #12: Tell your Supersymetric Mind to remove the right triangle from the space it currently occupies in the left triangle. You do not have to do anything else. No more concentration on a triangle base, or on the top of a triangle.
Your Supersymetric Mind knows what to do.
It will follow your command.
And instantly, the right triangle is separated from the left triangle. See illustration # 6.

*** *** ***

Reading peoples' thoughts

Illustration # 5

Reading peoples' thoughts

Illustration # 6

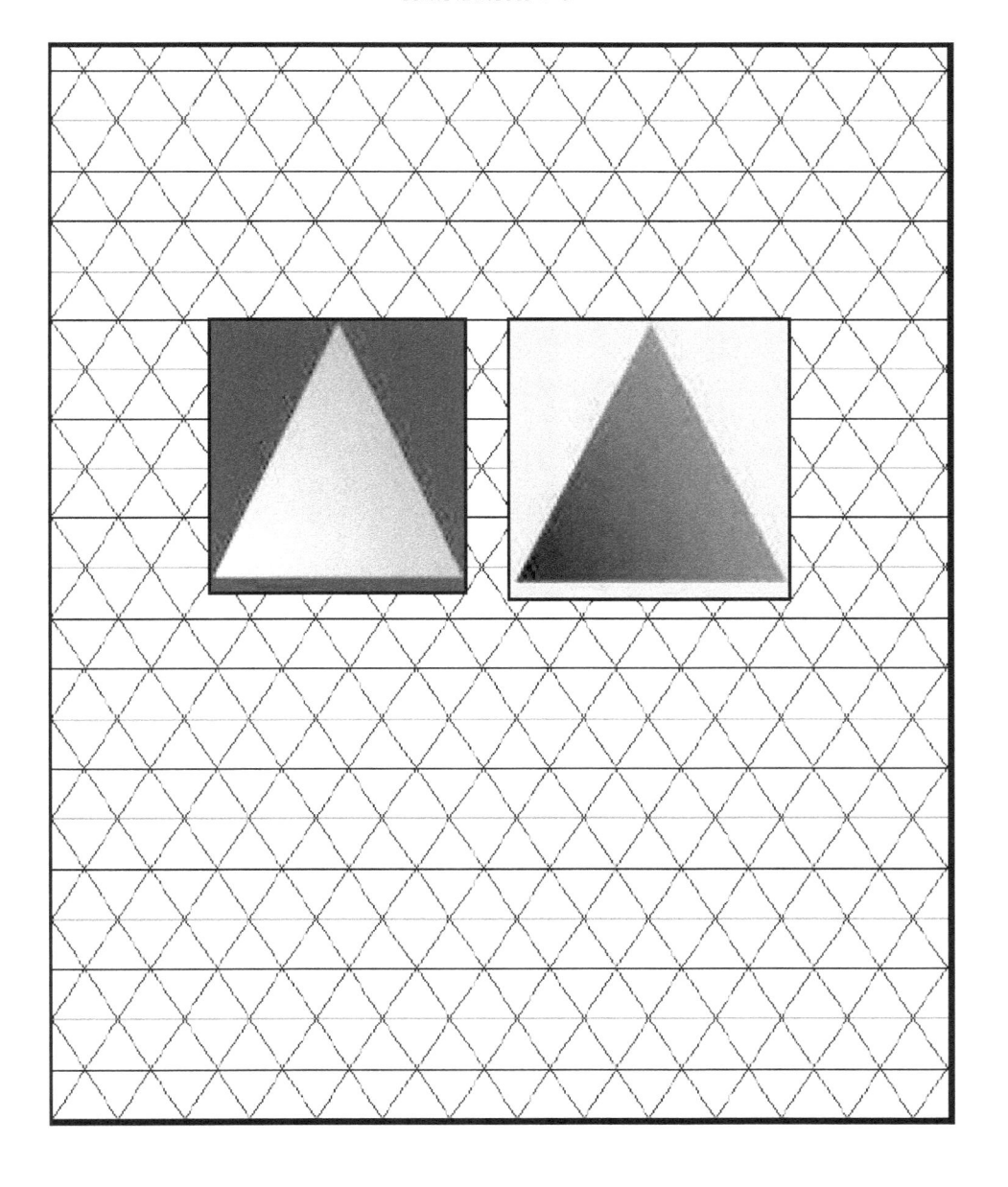

Step #13: Ask your Supersymetric Mind to move the left triangle closer to the right triangle, and merge partially with it.
See illustration #7.

Step #14: Ask your Supersymetric Mind to totally merge the left triangle with the right triangle.
I mean almost totally.
See illustration #8.

Step #15: Final exercise:
Ask your Supersymetric Mind to separate both triangles and bring them to their initial position on the grid.
See illustration #9.

You are done!
Congratulations! You have successfully completed the mental exercise of Iama/Takaroob.

*** *** ***

Reading peoples' thoughts

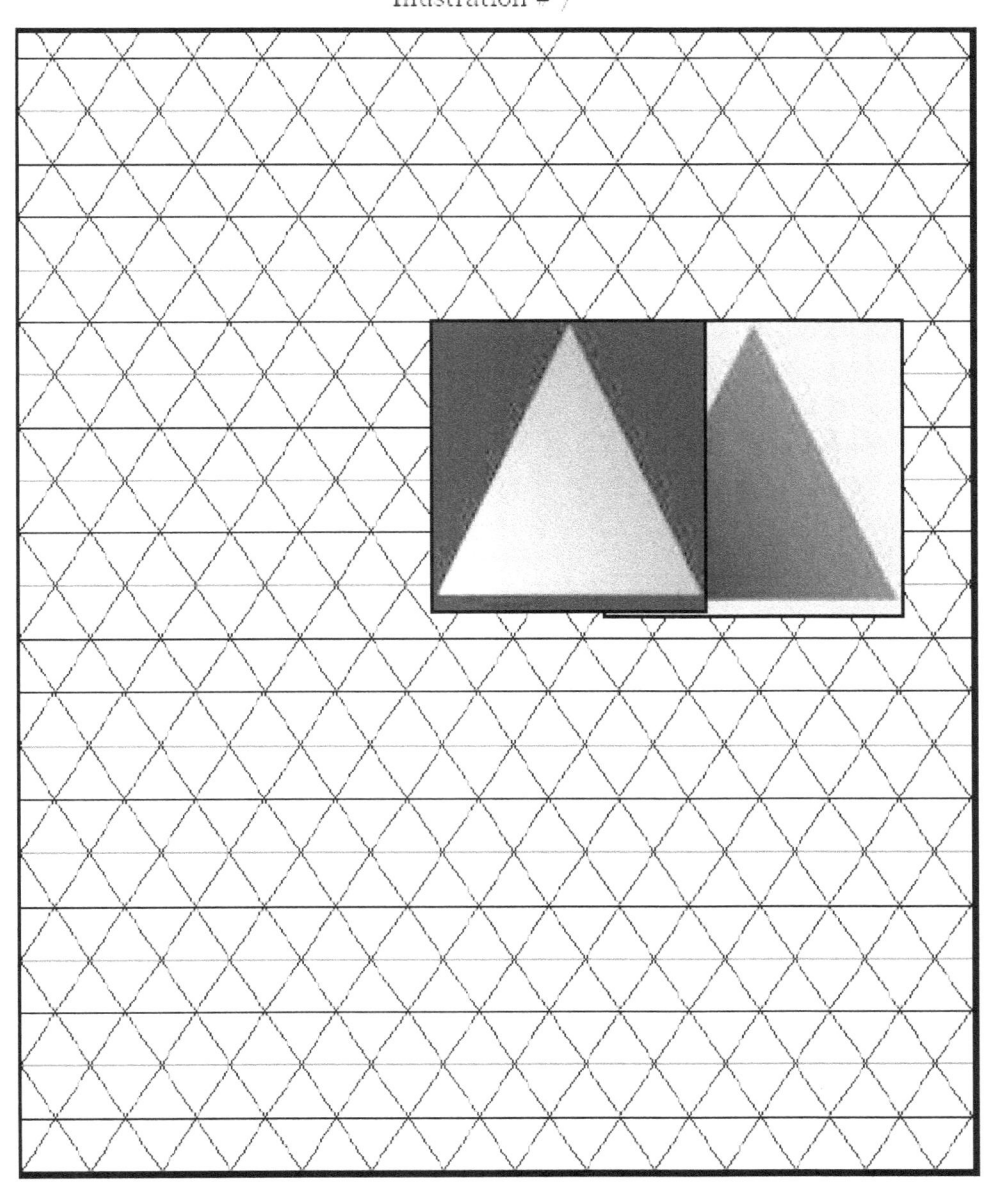

Illustration # 7

Reading peoples' thoughts

Illustration # 8

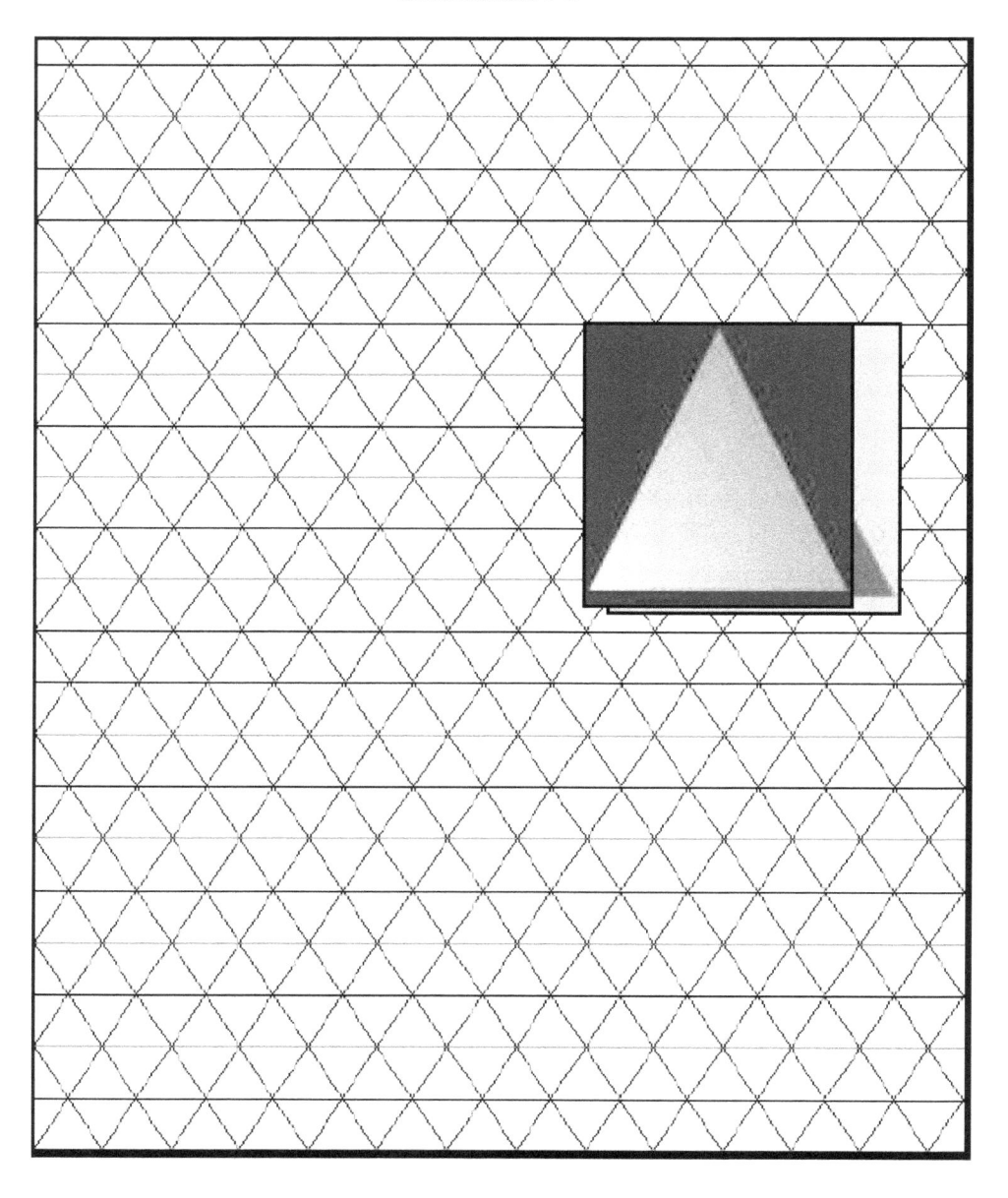

Reading peoples' thoughts

Nizraat Takaroob Technique
Illustration #9

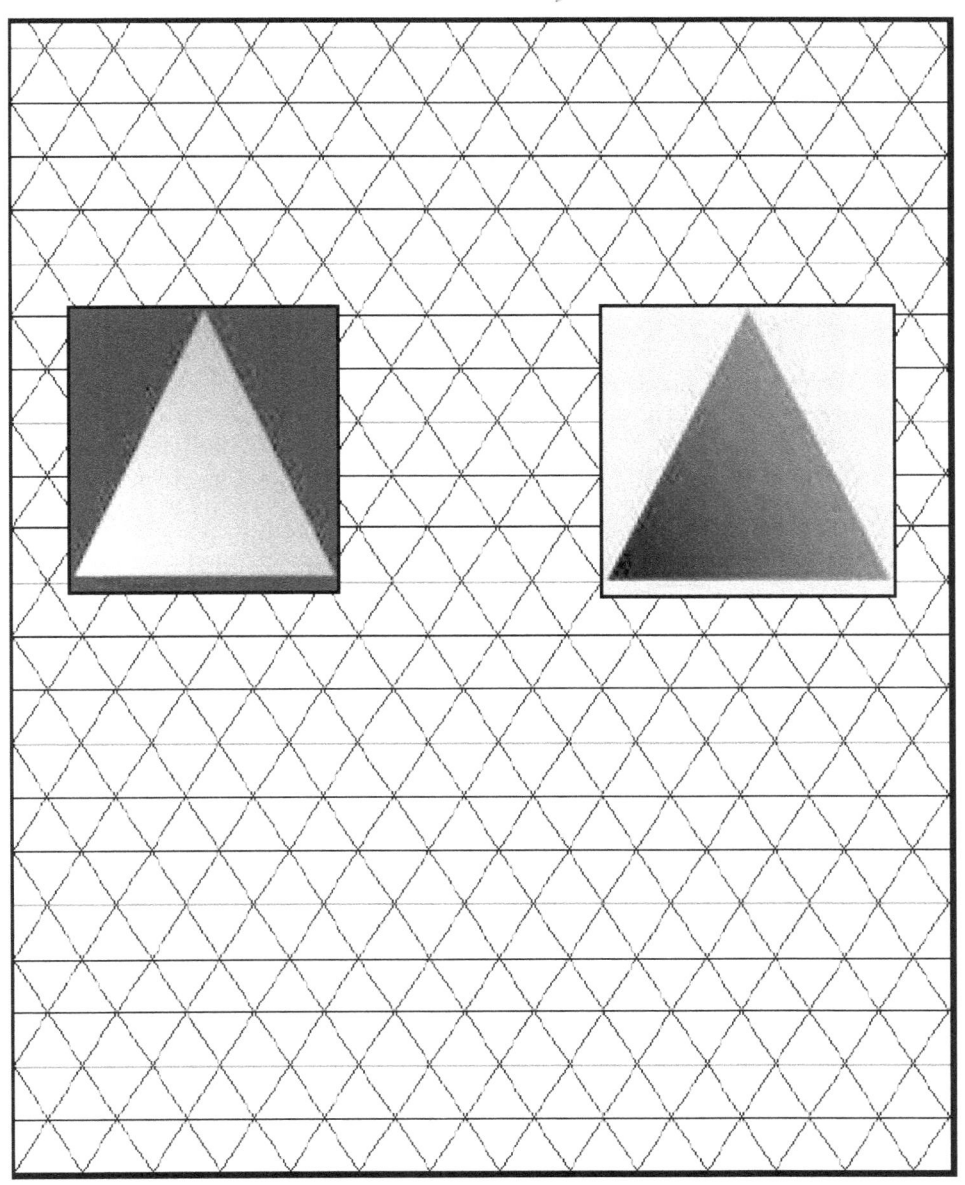

V. The benefits from mastering the Nizraat Takaroob technique

What have we accomplished so far by mastering the Ulema Nizraat Takaroob technique?
Why this mental exercise is necessary?
How can we benefit from it?
Well, first of all, you have to do something to trigger the Supersymetric Mind. In order to do so, you must transpose your "regular" mind to Ira'ha, which means a state of neutrality, in order to transpose the thoughts of others to your mental grid.
As long as your "regular" (Normal) mind is preoccupied with other things, significant or not, it can't liberate itself from those things, and reach a higher level of awareness. Meditation and introspection are always useful, but in this context, they would not help you to read others' thoughts, and to partially activate your Supersymetric Mind (SM). You have to remember that only through your SM you will be able to read others' mind.
The Nizraat Takaroob technique opens the Ma bira-rach, which is the etheric image of your brain (Mind). Once the Ma bira-rach, becomes accessible, other images will follow, and a wider mental perception expands. And these images bring to your mind, the thoughts of others.
The expansion of a wider mental perception frees your "regular" mind, and allows it to receive an avalanche of visions, messages, and ideas. In other words, you are retrieving, scanning, and storing all sorts of ideas and thoughts generated by others' mind.
In addition, the expansion of a wider mental perception superposes the Araya (Net of the mind) of your physical mind and the Araya of your Supersymetric Mind (Your other mind that exists as a bulk of separate particles in an etheric substance.)
And when this happens, you will have instant access to an amazingly vast depot of knowledge and information.
In addition to moving one triangle from one place to another one, (Which could seem silly to some!) your mind has learned now how to switch on and off an ordinary mind, and listen to frequencies, waves, and vibrations that contain extraordinary information about others.

Each time you transpose and scan others' thought (One at the time) you learn more about others.

Nizraat Takaroob adds an extra dimension of knowledge, information, and awareness to your "regular" Mind. Information about others, and especially reading their mind strengthens your position, and allows you to consider and evaluate all the possibilities, even foresee the outcome and consequences of your decisions.

And awareness makes you alert, keeps you in harmonious synchronization with your environment, and what is going on around you.

Once, you have mastered the Nizraat Takaroob technique, you will be able to apply it pragmatically in all your endeavors, including business transactions, planning, communication, decision making, rapports with others, and remote viewing.

*** *** ***

Chapter 6
The Practical Aspect of Reading Peoples' Thoughts Via Iama Technique

---

In theory, the technique sounds fascinating.
But does it work in real life? And can we use it in remote viewing and locating missing persons?
How can we use it to read people's mind?
First of all, the technique works perfectly. It has been used for centuries by seers and spiritual masters. Of course, it is not an easy task, for esoteric techniques require patience, an extended period of time and lots of practice.
I am going to show you step-by-step how to use it to read others' thoughts, and apply it in remote viewing.

I. Introduction: Generalities.
Before you start exploring the mechanism of the technique, you must learn and understand the symbolism and esoteric meaning of each element of the technique.

1-The Supersymetric Mind (SM): You will not be using your "normal" mind, the one you are familiar with, the one you read about in science books. Instead, you will use the SM, once it is activated. I can't for now dissert on the activation of the SM, because it requires a whole volume to explain how the SM works. Thus, you should refer to my book "Activation of the Conduit and the Supersymetric Mind." However, the nature of the SM has been briefly explained in this book, and this should help.

2-The landscape of the SM: You have to visualize the SM or simply your mind as a flat surface. On this surface float thoughts, ideas, feelings, emotions, intentions, etc; it is similar the surface (Rectangle) we have used in remote viewing, where you gather all your images and projections of things, objects, places and faces of people. Thus, the surface of your mind is similar to the surface of others' minds. But what it is different are others' thoughts, ideas and feelings. And together we shall be focusing on these thoughts, ideas and feelings.

3-On the surface of others' minds, their thoughts, ideas and feelings are represented by triangles. Thus, each one of their thoughts and ideas is represented by one single triangle. So while you are looking at somebody, and/or at his/her photograph, you should focus only on one idea at the time, meaning only on one of his or her thoughts and ideas.

4-Your mind at that particular moment should be clear, meaning don't think about anything else except reading (Guessing) his/her mind.

5-If the person remains silent: Anything he/she is thinking about takes shape in the form of a triangle. And it is this particular triangle you will attempt to bring to your grid.
Grid means the surface of your mind.

6-If the person is talking: Focus on the first words or the first sentence he/she pronounces.

7-Illustration #1 the Grid: The grid represents the total surface of the mind. The Grid contains a great number of triangles. And each triangle represents one single thought or idea. It is obvious you can't focus on all the triangles.

Thus, one single triangle for now must be considered.
But which one? Because you are still a beginner, select either the "Up Triangle", or the "Down Triangle". Don't worry how the triangle is going to function, how the grid will operate, and how your mind is going to process all the information.
If you have practiced enough on the Iama technique, your SM is already familiar with all these activities. Your SM will take care of all these maneuvers.

II. The technique: It works like this.
1. The person is standing in front of you: Consider him/her an easy target. And since he/she is not aware of what you are going to do (Reading his/her mind), you will be able to penetrate his/her mind at ease, unless he/she reads first your mind and blocks his/her mental grid (Surface of the mind).

2. Look at the person straight in the eyes, and immediately visualize him/her as a grid.

3. At the same time instruct your SM to read the person's mind. More precisely tell your SM to catch what the person is thinking about at that very particular moment.

4. You can accomplish that task by mentally sending a triangle to the person's mind. In fact, you are sending the triangle to the grid of his/her mind. Remember, the grid is the depot of all the thoughts of the person you are looking at. It is like if you are sending a robot to scan an area. The triangle will position itself on the grid. Don't ask how the triangle will manage to do that.
Your SM is working for you. He is your agent.
He is the robot who knows what to do. You don't have time to worry about this, because you got to catch fast, almost instantly what the person is thinking about. OK!

5. Now tell you mind to anchor the triangle on the left side of the grid. You have to remember that the Grid represents the person you are looking at. In other words, you have transformed the person into a Grid!
If you manage to do that, the person is yours!!
Well, you should be able to do that if you have succeeded in Step #3, and Step #4.

6. Now you send mentally a second triangle to the grid of the person you are looking at. You command the triangle to sit next to the first triangle. Position your triangle on the right side of the first triangle. See Illustration #1 of Nizraat Takaroob Technique.

7. Tell your SM to empty the content of the first triangle into the second triangle. The first triangle is his/hers, the second is yours. Note: I know what you are thinking of!! You are telling yourself, it is going to take long time to do all this, and by now the person is gone! Yes, it is true, the person has left and you didn't accomplish a thing. It is going to happen in your earlier attempts, but eventually, you will manage to visualize the Grid, to send the first triangle, to send the second triangle, to position the second triangle and to empty the content of the first triangle into the second triangle in a fraction of a second, when you become good

at it. This is why you have to keep on practicing until you do it right. It will take time, but practice makes perfect.

8. The first triangle you have sent is now dumping into the second triangle what the person is thinking of.
It could be lots of different things, many thoughts, feelings, emotion, ideas, etc.
So you have to sort out all this material (Content) rapidly and align the person's thoughts, meaning putting them in order. This could be hard thing to do if the person thinks fast and has a lot of things on his/her mind.
But don't worry we have a solution for this minor problem.
Apply what you have learned from Step #8. Here it is: "You concentrate on the very top of the right triangle." That's right. Just focus on the upper part of the triangle.
See below:

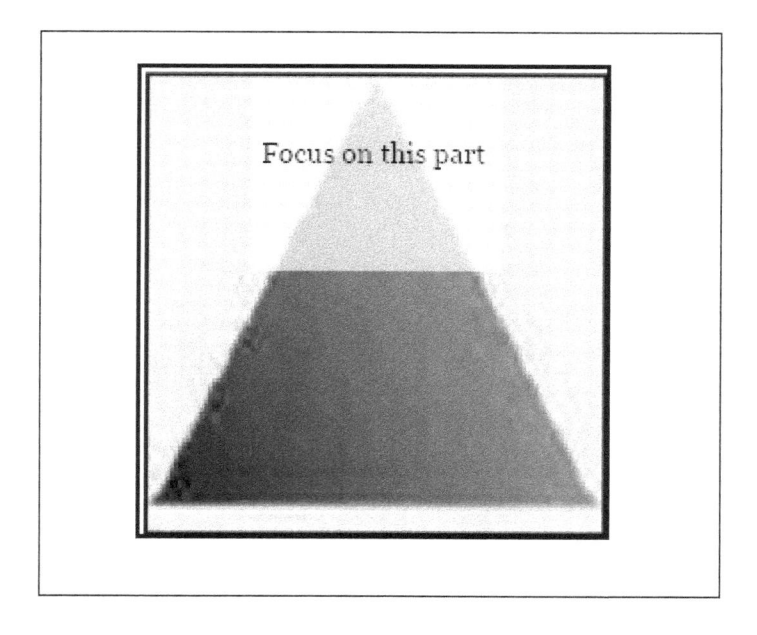

Focus on this part

9. The concentration on the top of the triangle organizes all the content dumped from the first triangle.
But because you are still a beginner, your concentration will scan only the very first thought of the person.
And that's not bad at all, because this is exactly what you wanted; to know his/her first thought.
Knowing the first thought should be helpful because it could serve you as a warning, as a revelation of the most important thing he/she is thinking about, and especially an information on what the person thought of you in the first place, what impression you have made on him/her, and how the person is reacting or feeling without telling you.

10. Ok, you got his/her thought.
But how to read it?
Very simple. A piece of cake.
As soon as your SM lists his/her first thought on the upper part of the triangle, your SM will instantly transmit it to your brain.
And how your brain will receive the transmission?
Illustration #8 provides the answer. I will explain:
Your SM erases the first triangle. More precisely it absorbs it. In other words, both triangles merge together.
But since your own triangle (The second triangle) becomes stronger than the first triangle because it is charged by the SM, everything found in your triangle becomes clearer, and consequently your mind will be able to see it and read it.
Call it if you want an inner telepathic message. In other words, you are communicating with yourself. It is exactly like when you usually think about something, anything.
You don't see what you are thinking about, you don't ask your mind to tell you what you are thinking about, you just think (Silently) and you get it right away.
It is already inside your mind.
I know you didn't expect this kind of explanation, but this is how the message is sent and received by you.
As you begin to learn more about Iama/Takaroob, you will discover so many wonderful things. And none of them is supernatural or magical.
It is simply the work and product of the "Transmission of Mind", a technique used for centuries by Middle Eastern mystics as well as by Zen masters.

In the future, and following your continuous training and practice, you will be able to read almost all the thoughts of others. But this phenomenal mental faculty will vanish if you use it for ill purposes.

I want you to succeed and you will.
And if you need help and additional guidance just email me. I am here for you. And remember, the most beautiful thing in the world is to find the pleasure in the pleasure of giving.
Walk in the light my friends and spread love, warmth and beauty around you.
It's time to go…so long.

*** *** ***

American Federation of Certified Psychics and Mediums Incorporated

---

The Legal Status of the Federation:
The American Federation of Certified Psychics and Mediums Incorporated is organized and incorporated under the laws of the State of New York. The Federation is to be a state registered corporation with the New York State Department of State in Albany New York, and as defined in subparagraph (a) (5) of Section 102 of the Not-for-Profit Corporation Law and Section 404 of the Not-For-Profit Corporation Law.

The Federation is organized as a New York Domestic Not-for-Profit corporation. It is organized exclusively for the purposes of developing, recognizing, certifying, and promoting the quality work of psychics and mediums via orientation programs, training, forums, discussions and public awareness, including for such purposes, the making of distribution to organizations that qualify as exempt organizations under Section 501 (c) (3) of the Internal Revenue Code, or the corresponding section of any future federal tax code.

The Purposes of the Federation are:
- 1-To promote the quality work of psychics and mediums.
- 2-To develop the abilities, talents and potentials of practitioners in the field.
- 3-To develop and conduct training programs and professional materials for the better advancement of psychics and mediums and their profession.
- 4-To grant official recognition and certifications for qualified psychics and mediums.
- 5-The public objective of the Federation is to help psychics and mediums explore and develop their full potentials and ameliorate their talents and gifts at no cost to them, and which without the help of the Federation, their work would and could not be acknowledged, made known and appreciated by the public.

Board of Directors Registered with the State of New York:
- Maximillien de Lafayette (Previously practiced law for 20 years), Founder and President,
- Dina Vitantonio, Secretary,
- Gideon Issa, Vice President,
- Elected by the Board: Aurele Issa, Treasurer,
- Elected by the Board: Patti Negri, Acting Chairwoman of the National Certifying Board, and Chief Examiner for the categoryof mediums and witchcraft.
- Shellee Hale, Chief Examiner for the category of Psychic detectives and missing persons.
- The Secretary of State is designated as agent of the Federation.

Members of the Board of State Directors and Regional Directors of the Federation's Chapters in the United States and abroad shall be announced following the first meeting of the Federation.

*** *** ***

The National Certifying Board:
The National Board consists of:
The president of the Federation
4 psychics or mediums for each category, chosen by the Federation (Depending on their category). The Examiners will administer the tests for each applicant on the phone, and in certain cases in person at a place designated by the Federation and/or the Examiners. The elected members are:
- Patti Negri, Acting Chairwoman, and Chief Examiner for the category of mediums and witchcraft.
- Shellee Hale, Chief Examiner for the category of Psychic detectives and missing persons.
- Dina Vitantonio, Examiner for the category of healers (Temporary Appointment).
- Maximillien de Lafayette, Member.
- Note: The Board is still reviewing applications to fill the positions of 3 remaining Examiners for the categories of: Psychics, Mediums, Healers.

Among the duties of the Board is to:

- 1-Administer Tests for applicants (Bona Fide practitioners with spotless reputation and documented ethical practice and accomplishments). The successful tests lead toward the granting of psychics and mediums National Certification/Recognition in their category (ies)
- 2-Oversee the Regional Directors (State Directors) of the Federation.

*** *** ***

Board of State Directors and Regional Directors: Members of the Board of State Directors and Regional Directors of the Federation's Chapters in the United States and abroad shall be announced following the first meeting of the Federation. The Federation shall have in each state in the United States of America, a State Director and/or a Regional Director, depending on the regional and structural needs of the Federation; this will:

- 1-Facilitate the mechanism of the Tests.
- 2-Respond to the local needs of psychics and mediums.
- 3-Process applications for membership.
- 4-Coordinate national and regional meetings, including the Annual National Convention.
- 5-Process and review complaints about psychics and mediums working in their states.

Membership into the American Federation of Certified Psychics and Mediums Incorporated

Membership Categories:

- **1-Associate Member:**

This is the first level of membership granted to applicants who are in the process of applying for professional certification which is awarded to all psychics and mediums who have passed the Proficiency Tests administered by Examiners, members of the National Certifying Board.

- **2-Certified Member:**

All applicants who have passed the Tests of the National Board are Board Certified Members.

Membership Fees/Dues:

- **Associate Member:**

There is a membership fee of $200 per year. This does not include the tests' fees.

- **Certified Member & Tests Fees:**

All applicants must take 2 tests administered by Examiners from The National Certifying Board. If they pass, they become Board Certified. Fees: $150. If they fail, the tests fees are not refundable.

- Membership's dues and tests' fees are not refundable

Upon submitting the request for membership, all applicants must submit the following documents:

- 1-Full name, telephone number and address (Residence and Office if applicable) including address of their website and emails.
- 2-A resume.
- 3-A detailed biography.
- 4-Clear statement about their refund policy.
- 5-Copies of their credentials (Certificates, Diplomas, etc). This is NOT a requirement, but it helps the National Board to get acquainted with the professional affiliation of the applicants. It is optional, since the Federation <u>does not recognize</u> and/or <u>accord</u> any value or importance to psychics/mediums credentials earned somewhere else.
- 6-No less than Twenty Five recommendations written by actual clients (Past or present). The recommendations must include the name of the clients and contact, for verification purposes.
- 7-A signed statement that the applicant was <u>never</u> convicted of any crime.
- 8-A signed statement that the applicant did not receive more than 2 complaints. If so, the applicant must elaborate further on this situation.

- 9-Applicants must agree to enroll in an Orientation Program (OP) for the development of their abilities. There is no cost, no fees and no tuitions for enrollment. Additional information on the OP will be provided to those who have passed the tests.
- 10-Applicants must agree to render at least one pro bono (Free of charge) service per year. This is part of their contributions to the community.

*** *** ***

Code of Ethics and Termination of Membership:

Members who violate the Code of Ethics and engage into unethical and illegal practices will be expelled from the Federation, and their membership will be terminated permanently. Violation of the rules and high standards of the Federation shall be determined by the Federation Board of Ethics and Fair Practice. Examples of acts that are considered a violation (To name a few):

- 1-Members' false claims and promises in any shape or form, including but not limited in advertisement, public speaking and communication with clients
- 2-Violation of their own refund policy
- 3-Badmouthing peers and colleagues
- 4-Misrepresentating facts
- 5-Use of fake credentials and titles
- 6-Causing physical, mental and emotional harm to clients and others
- 7-Commiting fraud and felonies

TESTS AND CERTIFICATION

The National Certifying Board consists of the president of the Federation, and two psychics or mediums chosen by the Federation (Depending on their category).

Administering the Tests (Generalities):

- 1-The Examiners will administer the tests for each applicant on the phone, and in certain cases in person at a place designated by the Federation and/or the Examiners.
- 2-Mediumship tests shall be conducted in the presence of a member of the National Certifying Board; in other words, mediumship tests (Evaluation, assessment and proficiency) cannot be conducted on the phone; no exception.
- 3-The method in which tests are administered by the Examiners is prescribed in the Federation Bylaws. This includes:
- a-The questionnaire,
- b-The demonstration of the psychic/medium abilities,
- c-The level of proficiency and accuracy, and
- d-Additional requirements and criteria defined by the National Certifying Board and approved by the Board of Directors of the Federation.

Duration of the tests:

Psychic Category:

- 1-Initial Test (First Test): 20 minutes on the phone.
- 2-Second Test administered by the President on the phone. Length: Undetermined.
- 3-Third Test (Challenge/Proficiency Test): Up to 60 minutes, whether on the phone or in person at a designated location.
- 4-The test is oral, written and field-trip related.
- 5-The examiners will report the results of the tests to the National Board.

Medium Category:

- 1-Initial Test (First Test/Interview): 20 minutes on the phone.
- 2-Second Test administered by the President on the phone. Length: Undetermined.

- 3-Third Test (Challenge/Proficiency Test): Duration to be determined by the Examiner.
- 4-Applicants will meet with the Examiner face to face at a designated location.
- 5-The Federation will designate Nationwide State Directors (NSD) and Nationwide Tests Examiners (NTE) to administer the tests and respond to the needs of the applicants.
- 6-The examiners will report the results of the tests to the National Board.

Essay: In addition, all applicants must submit a 10 to 15 page essay in a chosen field decided upon by the examiners and the applicant.

Documents to submit: Upon submitting the request for full membership (Certified Member Status), all applicants must submit the following documents:

- 1-Full name, telephone number and address (Residence and Office if applicable)
- 2-Address of their website and emails.
- 3-A detailed biography.
- 4-Clear statement about their refund policy.
- 5-Copies of their credentials (Certificates, Diplomas, etc). This is NOT a requirement, but it helps the National Board to get acquainted with the professional affiliation of the applicants. It is optional, since the Federation <u>does not recognize</u> and/or <u>accord</u> any value or importance to psychics/mediums credentials earned somewhere else.
- 6-No less than Twenty Five recommendations written by actual clients (Past or present). The recommendations must include the name of the clients and contact, for verification purposes.
- 7-A signed statement that the applicant was <u>never</u> convicted of any crime.
- 8-A signed statement that the applicant did not receive more than 2 complaints. If so, the applicant must elaborate further on this situation.

- 9-Applicants must agree to enroll in an Orientation Program (OP) for the development of their abilities. There is no cost, no fees and no tuitions for enrollment. Additional information on the OP will be provided to those who have passed the tests.
- 10-Applicants must agree to render at least one pro bono (Free of charge) service per year. This is part of their contributions to the community.

Certification:

- 1-Applicants who have successfully passed the tests in their category (ies) will receive the Certificate of "Certified Psychic" and/or "Certified Medium" corresponding to their category (ies).
- 2-An applicant can apply to a dual certification (Psychic and Medium). In this case, the applicant must take all the tests required for both categories.
- 3-There are no fees for receiving the proper certification (Getting the Certificates).
- 4-However, there are fees for taking the tests. (See Tests Fees)

Tests Fees for any category (Psychic or Medium):

- 1-One time fee of $150 for each category (Psychic or Medium)
- 2-All fees must be paid to the Federation before the tests are administered.
- 3-If the applicant fails, the tests fees are not refundable.

Asking for another test:

- 1-Those who have previously failed are allowed to take a second and last test.
- 2-Please contact the National Certifying Board for complete guidance and additional information.

Contact:

- President of the Federation: delafayette6@aol.com
- Secretary of the Federation: dinavitt@aol.com
- Chairwoman of the National Certifying Board: pinkkaire@aol.com
- Media: Shoshanna Rozenstein: newyorkgate@aol.com
- Consumers Protection Bureau: Peggy North: newyorkgate1@aol.com
- To apply for membership, email Maximillien de Lafayette, President of the Federation: delafayette6@aol.com

*** *** ***

New Books by Maximillien de Lafayette in these fields: Supernatural, Paranormal, Psychic studies, Mediumship, Remote Viewing, Healing, Energy, Tarot, Fortune-Telling, Clairvoyance
See products' details on page 191

- 1-How to Become an Enlightened Psychic, Medium and Metaphysical Master: Handbook of Curriculum, Lessons, Training, Supernatural Techniques and Powers, Foreseeing the future and psychic readings

- 2-The Register of the United States and World Best & Most Trusted Psychics, Mediums and Healers in International Rank Order 2012

- 3-How to Use Your Mind Power to do the Impossible: How to Positively Change your Future

- 4-How to Read Peoples' Vibes and Know Who They Really Are Just by Looking at Them (See their Aura, Sense their Vibes, Feel their Energy

- 5-Calendar of Hours & Days Which Bring You Bad & Good Luck: How to Positively Change your Future

- 6-Instructions and Techniques for Commanding Spirits and Communicating with Angels and Entities

- 7-Anunnaki Ulema Techniques and Tarot Deck To See Your Future. (The world's most powerful book on the occult and foreseeing your future on Earth and in other dimensions)

- 8-THE ESSENTIAL MAXIMILLIEN DE LAFAYETTE: The Official Anunnaki Ulema Textbook for the Teacher and the Student (The Road to Enlightenment and Ultimate Knowledge)

- 9-THE BOOK OF RAMADOSH: 13 Anunnaki Ulema Techniques to Live Longer, Happier, Healthier, Wealthier. 7th Edition.

- 10-HOW TO TALK TO SPIRITS, GHOSTS, ENTITIES, ANGELS AND DEMONS: Learn the Language of the Spirits and the Most Powerful Commands and Spells (Techniques and Instructions to communicate with the afterlife) 5th Edition.

- 11-How to Summon and Command Spirits, Angels, Demons, Afrit, Djinns. 3rd Edition. (Instructions and techniques on how to communicate with spirits)

- 12-Magical Talismans To Succeed In Life, Protect Yourself From Others And Summon Spirits.

- 13-The Complete Anunnaki Ulema Tarot Deck. Lessons And Techniques To See Your Future. 8th Edition. Volume 1 and Volume 2. The world's most powerful book on the occult and foreseeing your future on Earth and in other dimensions.

- 14-How to Acquire a Healing Touch (Lesson and Technique) Book/Lesson #5 (Lessons And Instructions On How To Acquire Anunnaki Ulema)

- 15-How to zoom into an astral body or in the Double.

- 16-Esoteric techniques to find the best & worst hours and days for your business, investment, love, relationships, success, wealth, and failure.

- 17-Esoteric techniques to reverse your bad luck, protect yourself against others vibes and find your lucky and unlucky days and hours. (Maps of cities, streets and neighborhoods that have negative currents and bad energy.)

- 18-How to block negative vibes and bad thoughts aimed at you

- 19-When Heaven Calls You: Connection with the Afterlife, Spirits, 4th Dimension, 5th Dimension, Higher-Self, Astral Body, Parallel Dimensions and Beyond the Future of Time and Space

*** *** ***

New Books by Maximillien de Lafayette in these fields

Website: www.maximilliendelafayettebibliography.com
Books available at barnes & noble, amazon.com, lulu.com and nationwide/worldwide

How to Use Your Mind Power to do the Impossible

How to Use Your Mind Power to do the Impossible" provides you with techniques that could help you discover, sense, and direct the power of your mind. Quite often, spiritual teachers, guides, channelers, psychics, mediums and healers talk about that un-je-ne-sais-quoi "Energy"! But rarely, do they explain in simple terms, what that energy is! What is made from? How energy is created? How energy could be sensed and directed? How to use it to create a positive environment? How to use energy to block others' negative thoughts and unhealthy energy? Can we see others' energy? Can we see our own energy? And, can we measure energy?

If pertinent answers and explanations are not given to us, then, kiss goodbye that energy, and all the mambo-jumbo lectures of the spiritual masters and so-called psychics. And, it's as simple as that. In order to develop the mental power of our mind, we must first, discover the energy of our mind and body. This discovery could be achieved through Ikti-Chafa, which the author has explained at length in the book. All of us possess what others call "supernatural powers." In fact, there is nothing "supernatural" at all. It is a matter of discovering and understanding how mental vibrations are created and transmitted. The book offers techniques which will enable you to use the power of your mind over matter. It is not an easy task, but it could be done if you practice and persevere. In addition to discovering and animating the power of your mind (Mental energy), you must absolutely understand how Mintaka Difaya works. Mintaka Difaya is related to "Protecting your Zone", the physical and mental zone that surrounds your body.Without such protection, our mental power will remain minimal. There is a wonderful technique in the book which will enable you to accomplish this task.

How to Read Peoples' Vibes and Know Who They Really Are Just by Looking at Them
(See their Aura, Sense their Vibes, Feel their Energy)

This is the first time ever, a step-by-step manual/book on how to read peoples' vibes and know who they really are just by looking at them has been published. A most useful and fascinating book that teaches you how to see peoples' Aura, sense their vibes, and feel their energy. It is abundant with illustrations, charts and sketches describing in detail all the phases and stages of fabulous Mind-Power esoteric techniques which were shrouded in secrecy for centuries. Just look at any person and find out in seconds what he/she is thinking of, what his or her intentions are, and how you can use effective techniques to: 1-Counter vicious thoughts and actions aimed at you. 2-Discover what people are thinking of you. 3-Read their mind and consequently adopt a successful strategy to boost your position, protect your interests, and enhance your communication skills. 4-Unlock the mysteries of the human mind, and use it as an effective tool to make your dreams come true.

The book is an unprecedented invitation to the world of Power of the Mind and its mysteries, a journey to another dimension where only the privileged seers and mystic Ulema could enter and learn from. It is a book of wisdom, Firasa and ultimate knowledge.

Calendar of Hours & Days Which Bring You Bad & Good Luck: How to Positively Change your Future

It includes:
• Factors which influence your future and luck
• The influence of the Anunnaki's programming of our brain and fate: A rare lecture on luck
• How to read Shashat; the screen of the unknown
• Rizmanah; Discover the calendar of your bad luck and good luck
• Learn how to remove your bad luck
• Learn how to create a good luck
• Daily chart/calendar of your good hours and bad

hours in your life
• What to do and not to do during these hours and these days
• Best hours and best days, worst hours and worst days for
• Employees
• Booksellers
• Writers
• Investment
• Real estate business
• looking for a new apartment
• Buying gold
• Buying hard currency
• Selling your art
• Asking for raise and promotion
• Stocks and Shares (trade, selling or buying)
• For writing/submitting proposals and grants
• Job applications
• Meeting new people
• Selling new ideas
• Opening a new business
• Signing contracts, etc…
• Importance of your name in shaping good luck
• Writing/equating your name in Ana'kh Phoenician
• How to write/transpose your name in the Sahiriin language
• Map of United States lucky and unlucky zones
• Case Study: Unhealthy energy and vibrations that damage you and negatively affect your future
• Esoteric techniques you could use to positively influence or improve your future and business by protecting yourself against evildoers
• Grid useful for business, negotiations, meetings
• Foreseeing your future is not enough. You must protect yourself as well. Learn how to do it.
• Grid "Ain Ali" to be used to prevent others from hurting you
• Going back in time and creating a brighter future.
• How real is the holographic/parallel dimension you are visiting in a different dimension?

Instructions and Techniques for Commanding Spirits and Communicating with Angels and Entities
Revised Edition of the previously published book "Magical Talismans To Succeed In Life, Protect Yourself From Others And Summon Spirits".
Paperback edition:

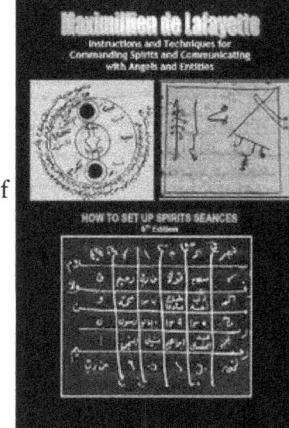

lulu.com/product/paperback/instructions-and-techniques-for-commanding-spirits-and-communicating-with-angels-and-entities/16962325. No doubt you will succeed in summoning some of the entities, spirits and presences, if you diligently comply with the rules, and follow the instructions of the Sahiriin and the Honorable Allamah as prescribed in this book. The Allamah told us that it is possible to contact them ONLY during the 40 day period following their death. The book will show you how to communicate with some of these entities, summon them, ask them favors, and even command them.

From the table of contents:
* 1.Learn the language of the Arwaah (Spirits)
* 2. Learn how to talk to entities, spirits, souls, presences
* 3. Learn how to befriend spirits.
* 4. Learn how to set-up a spirits séance
* 5.Materials and accessories you need for summoning and communicating with spirits and entities
* 6.Learn how to write/transpose your name in the Sahiriin language
* 7. Writing/Equating your name in Ana'kh/Proto-Ugaritic
* 8.Chart of the good hours to contact the spirits
* 9. Magical writing for preserving good health
* 10. Magical writing for multiple purposes: To triumph. To defeat your enemies. To stop black magic against you.
* 11. Magical writing to remove blocks and barriers. To free a prisoner. To heal a person hit by black magic and curses
* 12. Magical square for protection against the "Evil Eye", bad spirits, and envious/vicious people
* 13. Talisman against fear and a bullying boss
* 14. Magical writing against people who hate you
* 15. Magical writing against powerful people who could be a threat to you
* 16. Talabaat to influence others' decisions

Anunnaki Ulema Techniques and Tarot Deck To See Your Future. (The world's most powerful book on the occult and foreseeing your future on Earth and in other dimensions)
The world's most powerful book on the occult and foreseeing your future on Earth and in other dimensions.9th Edition. Previously published under "Ulema Anunnaki Tarot". Revised, Expanded and Indexed. For the first time ever in the Western world, and in the history of the occult, divination, Tarot,

Anunnaki, Ulema, and esoteric studies of all kinds, the reader, the seer, the adept and the novice will have access to the world's most powerful book on the subject. These 7,000 year old secrets, and forbidden knowledge and techniques, for reading the future and changing major events in your life, are being made available for the first time. Lessons, advice, techniques, training and reading your Future and Tarot are directly provided by the last contemporary Ulema Anunnaki who lived consecutively through three centuries. Techniques and lessons include how to discover your lucky hours and days; how to reverse bad luck; learning about your past lives, your present, your future, and your multiple existences on Earth and in other dimensions, how to foresee and avert imminent dangers threatening your life, health, career, business, and relationships. Tarot Anunnaki Ulema Bakht Kiraat is the study and reading of one's future on Earth and in other dimensions. It regroups the past into the present, and transcends the frontiers of the present to reach the realm of the future. The "Ulema Anunnaki Tarot: Lessons and Techniques to See your Future" is the first published work on foretelling your future day by day, hour by hour. There is no other book written on the subject. Bakht has been practiced by the Ulema Anunnaki for thousands of years. It is totally unknown in the Western hemisphere.

Essentially, Tarot Bakht is based upon knowledge received from the early remnants of the Anna.Ki, also called Anu.Na.Ki, an extra-terrestrial race which landed on Earth hundreds of thousands of years ago.

Very few seers and mystics outside the circle of the Ulema Anunnaki penetrated the secrets of the Bakht. They were the elite of the priests of Ra, the early Sinhar Khaldi (Early Chaldean priests, astrologers, astronomers), the Tahar (Early Phoenician Purification priests), and the Rouhaniyiin, known in the West as the alchemists/Kabalists. In the whole world today, there are no more 700 persons who practice the Bakht, and they are called Ba-khaat or Bakhaati. Two hundred of them are the supreme enlightened masters, called Mounawariin. The earliest manuscript on Bakht appeared in Phoenicia, circa 7,500 B.C., and it was written in Ana'kh. A later version in Anakh-Proto-Ugaritic appeared three thousand years later. A third version written in the early Phoenician-Byblos script appeared in Byblos and Tyre.

The book includes your Tarot Cards Deck.

From the contents:
• 1.Techniques for reading the future
• 2.Your future already exists in another dimension
• 3. Linear Future and Multidimensional Future
• 4.The origin, power and strength of your name, and how it affects your

present and future
- 5.Ismu Ardi; your name on Earth, the one your parents gave you
- 6.Ismu Khalka; your non-Earth name, the one the Anunnaki your creator gave you
- 7.How to find and write your name in Ana'kh, the Anunnaki language
- 8.The best time to read your future
- 9.On Earth, you are simply a copy of yourself
- 10.Recommended days and hours for reading your Tarot

THE ESSENTIAL MAXIMILLIEN DE LAFAYETTE: The Official Anunnaki Ulema Textbook for the Teacher and the Student (2 Volumes: Approx. 1500 Pages)

THE ESSENTIAL MAXIMILLIEN DE LAFAYETTE is a synopsis of the 200 books, the author wrote on the subjects of the Anunnaki, the afterlife, the supernatural powers of the Anunnaki Ulema, the paranormal, the occult, parallel dimensions, multiple universes, the Conduit, the Supersymetric Mind, the Double, the Astral Body, communications with spirits and entities from the world beyond, the power of the mind, mediumship, channeling, the enlightenment, the Fourth Dimension, the Fifth Dimension, Earth energy, healing, the world outside time and space, extraterrestrials, time-travel, reading the future, and similar topics. This is NOT a repetitious book. It was intentionally compiled from the most important concepts, theories, esoteric techniques, wisdom, Eastern philosophy, the world of the mystic seers "The Ulema", and particularly the teaching of Maximillien de Lafayette. This series consists of 2 massive volumes, each exceeding 700 pages (50 MB). This manual is also the Official Anunnaki Ulema Textbook for the Teacher and the Student. De Lafayette wrote more than 800 books, 200 of them are in these fields. Consequently, it is quasi-impossible for the reader to purchase all these books. The present work contains knowledge, techniques and revelations, no other author has ever discussed, simply because they emerge from the teachings of the author's Enlightened Masters and his own philosophy. Add to the fact, that no other author or researcher has ever approached these topics, simply because they were brought to the West, for the first time in history, from the author's own vision and perspective. You will NOT find the material of this book in any other work, and/or in any library. As a matter of fact, the material of the present work (Volumes 1 and 2) is to a certain degree in sharp contrast with what it has been said or written in these fields. No one can claim that this book was inspired by or based upon any existing published book. It is a journey to new dimensions, and analysis of the physical and mental worlds as interpreted personally by the author. The contents include:1. Description of the Afterlife in all its states and dimensions. 2. What do we see when we enter the afterlife zone? 3. The various states of metamorphosis of the mind-body of a deceased person in the after-life. 4. Experiences dead people encounter in the next dimension. 5. How to bring good luck to your endeavors and surmount obstacles and hardship that prevent you from succeeding in life. 6. How to use Earth energy to your advantage and block others' bad vibes and vicious intentions that are causing you harm and damage. 7. The first stage of the afterlife during the 40 day period following death, and how to communicate with your departed loved ones and pets. 8. How the Anunnaki created us genetically 65,000 years ago. 9. The mysterious and hidden world of the Anunnaki Ulema as the author knew it and explored it. 10. Foreseeing the future and rewinding time; revisiting your childhood and past life in different dimensions. 11. How the Masters, the Mounawiriin, and the Anunnaki Ulema transpose you from the present to the future? 12. How to develop The Supersymetric Mind. 13. Study of the influence of the Anunnaki's programming of our brain and fate. 14. The duplicate image of ourselves or reproduction of our body in other dimensions. 15. The early human species and races created by the extraterrestrials. 16. How to learn The Anunnaki Ulema supernatural and mind power techniques. 17. Entering a parallel dimension; Is it possible to enter a parallel dimension and leave there all your troubles? YES! 18. Occult techniques and talismans to protect yourself from others. And much much more.-By Dina Vittantonio, Editor.

HOW TO TALK TO SPIRITS, GHOSTS, ENTITIES, ANGELS AND DEMONS: Learn the Language of the Spirits and the Most Powerful Commands and Spells (Techniques and Instructions to communicate with the afterlife) 5th Edition.

Practical and simplified techniques to create a mediumship séance and communicate with the dead, spirits, angels, demons, departed pets, and entities from the after-life. This book will change your life and your understanding of the afterlife, for ever. It is your link to the other world, the realm of the spirits, angels, ghosts, and demons. It provides the necessary guidance and techniques to communicate with various categories of entities. It instructs the seeker how to comply with rules and pre-requisites to follow during a séance. The author has placed a strong emphasis on: The language of the spirits & ghosts, The most powerful commands we can use during a séance, and how to order the summoned entities to grant us most needed favors and assistance in urgent matters, as well as general commands pertaining to health conditions, the removal of difficulties in getting a job, the protection of our home from evil spirits, obtaining an immediate financial relief, so on. This book provides both the experienced and the beginner with the necessary guidance, ways and techniques to communicate with various kinds and categories of entities. The author has placed a strong emphasis on: The language of the spirits, ghosts, entities and Arwaah. What should we do when we hear the voices of entities during a séance? The reader should pay attention to the instructions pertaining to a direct conversation with summoned entities, and especially to the protocol in communicating with spirits. This is the first book ever published in the West that deals with these topics. The contents and ideas presented in this tome are based upon the teachings and lectures of enlightened masters, who have practiced this etheric art for centuries. Therefore, you should open your mind, and read this book with extreme attention to the instructions provided by the Ulema. Contacting spirits and entities is a serious responsibility. They will respond to you if you follow the spirits' protocol, as explained in the book.

It includes:
1. Learn the language of spirits, ghosts, entities and Arwaah
2. What should we do when we hear the voices of the spirits?
3. Most powerful commands.
4. Command to improve your health condition.
5. Command to remove difficulties in getting a job.
6. Command to obtain the affection or attention of a person you are interested in.
7. Command to protect your home from evil spirits.
8. Command to win a favorable verdict.
9. Command to free you promptly from detention.
10. Command to obtain immediate financial relief.
11. Command to help you in your business and bring more customers.
12. Command to succeed in a new business or a joint-venture.
13. Command to get a promotion.
14. Gallery of ghosts/spirits/orbs photos: The fake and the real.
15. What is the spirits and ghosts protocol "Nizam Arwaah"?
16. Can we contact our departed parents through our double? And is it dangerous to contact the dead?
17. Is it possible to visit the world beyond?
18. What would happen to us when we return to earth after exiting the

4th dimension?
19.What is the 4th dimension? Where is the 4th dimension?
20.Is it possible to enter the realm of spirits/ ghosts, instead of summoning them? 21.What do we see when we enter another dimension, such as the realm of spirits, or a parallel world?
22.Can I use my native language to talk to ghosts and spirits? Do spirits, ghosts and other entities understand foreign languages?
23.How should I start a conversation with a ghost or a spirit?
24.Can I take pictures of ghosts and spirits just to make sure that they do exist?
25.Is it possible to summon the ghost or spirit of a dead relative?
26.Is it possible to communicate with dead pets? Yes.

Magical Talismans To Succeed In Life, Protect Yourself From Others And Summon Spirits.
3rd Edition (Instructions and techniques on how to communicate with spirits)

Volume 2 (Final Part) of the series: How to summon and command spirits, angels, demons, afarit, Djinns. Title of Volume I is: How to Summon and Command Spirits, Angels, Demons, Afrit, Djinns. The book is inspired by the Anunnaki-Ulema, Allamah, and Sahiriin. Absolutely brand new information never revealed before, or mentioned in any book in the West or the East. There is no other book like it on earth! It is the world's first, most useful and most powerful book on how to communicate with spirits, and summon angels, demons, entities and creatures from this world and the one beyond. It reveals the real techniques of magic and spirits summoning instructions shrouded in secrecy for 1,700 years.

This volume includes:
1.Language of the Spirits and how to talk to a summoned entity.
2.Magical writings to triumph, defeat your enemies, and stop black magic against you.
3.Magical square for protection against the "Evil Eye", bad spirits, and envious/vicious people.
4.Talisman against fear and a bullying boss.

5. Magical writing against powerful people who could be a threat to you.
6. Magical writings for summoning the most powerful spirits.
7. How to use Daa-irat Al Shams Al Koubra and reverse your bad luck.
8. You, your life, your success, the Parallel Lines, and the spirits who control your fate.

The Complete Anunnaki Ulema Tarot Deck. Lessons And Techniques To See Your Future. 8th Edition. Volume 1 and Volume 2. The world's most powerful book on the occult and foreseeing your future on Earth and in other dimensions.

Tarot Anunnaki Ulema Bakht Kiraat is the study and reading of one's future on Earth and in other dimensions. It regroups the past into the present, and transcends the frontiers of the present to reach the realm of the future. The "Ulema Anunnaki Tarot: Lessons and Techniques to See your Future" is the first published work on foretelling your future day by day, hour by hour. There is no other book written on the subject. Bakht has been practiced by the Ulema Anunnaki for thousands of years. It is totally unknown in the Western hemisphere. Essentially, Tarot Bakht is based upon knowledge received from the early remnants of the Anna.Ki, also called Anu.Na.Ki, an extra-terrestrial race which landed on Earth hundreds of thousands of years ago. Very few seers and mystics outside the circle of the Ulema Anunnaki penetrated the secrets of the Bakht.

They were the elite of the priests of Ra, the early Sinhar Khaldi (Early Chaldean priests/astrologers/astronomers), the Tahar (Early Phoenician Purification priests), and the Rouhaniyiin, known in the West as the alchemists/Kabalists. In the whole world today, there are no more 700 persons who practice the Bakht, and they are called Ba-khaat or Bakhaati. Two hundred of them are the supreme enlightened masters, called Mounawariin. The earliest manuscript on Bakht appeared in Phoenicia, circa 7,500 B.C., and it was written in Ana'kh. A later version in Anakh-Pro-Ugaritic appeared three thousand years later. A third version written in the early Phoenician-Byblos script appeared in Byblos and Tyre.

The book includes:
Do we have one future or multiple futures?
Are we trapped in this life?
Are we the slaves of a Supreme Creator?.
Can we change our future and create our own destiny, without upsetting God?
Can Bakht reading help us free ourselves and learn about our future?
Your name
Ismu Ardi; your name on Earth
Ismu Khalka; your name in other dimension.
How can I find my true name (Code); the one the Anunnaki gave me before I was born? YES!!
Techniques and chart for the best time to read your future
Recommended days and hours for reading your Bakht
The book has a complete Tarot deck, and shows you how to use it.
Is it true some places or neighborhoods bring bad luck? The deck will tell you.
Is it true bad spirits can manifest themselves while reading the Bakht? The deck will tell you.
What do I need to put exactly in the Bakht reading to find out information about a person I am interested in? I want to know everything about that person? Is it possible? YES!!

Register of the United States and World's Best and Most Trusted Psychics, Mediums and Healers in International Rank Order

Listing 855 names. Published by UFOs & Supernatural Magazine. Hard copy paperback (book 406 pages, size: 8 inches x 10 inches) can be ordered at newyorkgate@aol.com This is the world #1 reference source, and most authoritative book on the most reliable, trusted mediums & healers around the globe. They are included in the Register because they were chosen, nominated & recommended by the public & their clients. They are the PEOPLE'S CHOICE. This is the world's first book/register of its kind, compiled and written by independent researchers and reporters who have no ties to any psychic, medium, healers and related agencies.
The book includes
The Good, the Bad, the Ugly
The good ones and those who made a wonderful impression on me
Trashing each others
Ego bigger than the Empire State Building
Don't worry about what others might say about you if it is not true. Worry only, if it is true
Sympathizing with harassed psychics, mediums and healers
Fake credentials
Chapter 1: Revealing Statistics: Profession and way of life of psychics
Chapter 2: Brief Analysis of Clients' Emails of Recommendations
Chapter 3: Results of the 1st Annual National Vote/Election of America's Best Psychics 2012
Category: America's Best Psychics in National Rank Order
Category: America's Most Famous/Popular Psychics in National Rank Order
(LISTING OVER 850 NAMES) Chapter 4: The World's Best and Most Trusted Psychics, Mediums and Healers in an International Rank Order
Top ten in the world in international rank order: The world very best and most trusted
Top twenty in the world
Top thirty in the world
Top forty in the world
Top fifty in the world
Top sixty in the world
Top seventy in the world
Psychics, Mediums, Healers, Numerologists, Astrologers, Spiritual Advisors, Etc. Recommended by the general public from 126 countries: By Name and Category in Alphabetical Order Starting with their First Name
Chapter 5: Rapport with Top Psychics, Mediums, Healers
What we felt. Our own feelings & perceptions on a scale of 1 to 10
Chapter 6: Samples of clients' recommendations and testimonies
Chapter 7: Best Refund Policies
Chapter 8: Profiles of distinguished psychics, mediums & healers

Facts: A message from the author.

1-I did not select psychics, mediums and healers for my book. As a matter of fact 98% of them are unknown to me. Their clients in the thousands recommended them and voted for them. They would send me emails containing their full names, what they do for a living, their websites to be included in the book, and describe their experiences with said lightworkers. As a matter of fact, I stated very clearly in the book, that I do NOT recommend any one (In the book or elsewhere) to be a perfect lightworker and/or a spiritual teacher. Thus the clients and the general public voted; NOT ME!

2-The vote was a long process; the clients and the general public continued to vote around the clock, non-stop for 25 days. Almost the whole psychics-mediums' community knew about the vote. And if they didn't know despite the lengthy process of 25 days, then one thing comes to my mind: THEY ARE NOT PSYCHIC!!!

3-I did not pass a judgment on the 855 listed lightworkers. Never, ever. Only on 4 pages, I described the kind of conversations I had with approx. 15 of them, and what vibes I received from communicating with them. I spoke briefly (2 lines or 3) about 15 only, and not 855!!!!

4-Zillions of affidavits, statements and letters/emails of recommendation from clients and the general public (Doctors, professors, authors, psychics, scientists, heads of corporations, superstars who sent me their emails are mentioned in the book.)

5-Those who were elected are the very best in the business. To mock them is a vicious and low-class attempt to dishonor them and attack their credibility. Any person who would slander them is nothing but the scum of the earth. Hatred, jealousy, envy, ignorance and fear of competition will motivate many to hurt others and discredit the book. But they will fail, for the PUBLIC HAS VOTED, and the TRUTH is revealed. I do strongly believe that Michelle Whitedove, Patti Negri, Allison Hayes, Chinhee & Sunhee Park, Shellee Hale, Danielle Egnew, Gabriela Castillo, Patrice Cole, Micki Dahne, Syd Saeed, Claire Braddock, Russell Grant, Lynne Caddick, Tina Bliss, Barbara MacKey, Melissa Bacelar, Bee Herz, Maureen Hancock, Dolores Cannon, Suzanne Grace, Ali Michaels, Blair Robertson, Bobby Marchesso, Brian Hunter, Chip Coffey, Daved Beck, Dougall Fraser, Doyle Ward, James Van Praagh, Jamie Clark, Jeffry Palmer, Jerry Yusko, Jethro Smith, John Edward, John Holland, Justin Chase Mullins, Matt Fraser, Robert Valera, Steven Weiss and so many others who were voted by the public and included in the book are de facto, among the best in the world, if not, the best of the very best.

6-No lightworker has ever paid a dime to be included or listed in the book, as owners of websites that list psychics on the Internet do and keep on doing. They charge psychics from $50 to $99 per month. I found this, to be atrocious and unfair.

7-I have no ties to any psychic or medium. I have no interest in their financial enterprises. I was not paid to write about them. None of my assistants and investigative reporters is part of their circles and businesses.

8-Already owners of websites that list psychics for a fee began to wage a war against my book, the honored psychics in the book, and even my name and integrity. They think that I am a threat to them, a real competition that could diminish their income, generated by fees paid by psychics, to be listed on their websites. I list psychics free. They list them for a fee. And if they cease to pay the listing fees, they kick them out!!!! They are strictly business people.

9-In summary, the book was written, compiled and produced -by large- by myself, thousands of clients and unbiased reporters.

10-Venomous so-called reviews of the book will surface soon, here and elsewhere, and to those who found satisfaction in doing so, I will say: les chiens aboient, la caravane passe.

11-I asked the readers to be indulgent in the case they find grammatical errors in the emails, statements and recommendations of the clients. Some showed understanding and compassion. Few bitterly pointed out that the book is full of grammatical mistakes and errors. Well, they are not mine for sure. However few typos I hold myself responsible for. It is a huge book which exhausted me for almost 2 months non-stop. So please turn the other cheek instead of biting me.

12--I am so grateful to amazon.com and thousands of friends, psychics and readers who made this book a bestseller in less than 24 hours! Thank you.

*** *** ***

AMERICA's & WORLD's BEST PSYCHICS & HEALERS WHO CARE MOST ABOUT YOU
Names, Profiles, Services, Rates, Contact

It includes:
- Lightworkers Specialty and Area of Practice
- Listing of Practitioners by their First Name

- Listing by Specialty and Area of Practice
- Listing of Lightworkers and Practitioners by State or Location
- Rates and Fees
- Listing: From the Lowest to the Highest
- Rates and names of practitioners
- Psychics, Mediums and Lightworkers Best and Very Best Refund Policy
- Hall of Fame of the Most Caring Lightworkers
- Psychics, Mediums and Lightworkers Who Were Recommended by Psychics, Mediums and Lightworkers
- Psychics, Mediums and Lightworkers who were recommended by the general public
- Testimonies and Recommendations for lightworkers and practitioners
- Interview with the best of the best in the business
- Psychics, Mediums, Healers and Lightworkers TV and Radio Shows:
- The Best on the Air

NOTES

NOTES

Published by
Times Square Press
WJNA, Inc.
UFOs & Supernatural Magazine
New York, New York, USA

Printed in the United States of America
March 2012

www.ingramcontent.com/pod-product-compliance
Ingram Content Group UK Ltd.
Pitfield, Milton Keynes, MK11 3LW, UK
UKHW012103060625
6284UKWH00014B/121